A Family Resource Guide on International Parental Kidnapping

A Family Resource Guide on International Parental Kidnapping

U.S. Department of Justice
Office of Justice Programs
Office of Juvenile Justice and Delinquency Prevention

**Fredonia Books
Amsterdam, The Netherlands**

A Family Resource Guide on International Parental Kidnapping

by
U.S. Department of Justice

ISBN: 1-4101-0814-7

Copyright © 2005 by Fredonia Books

Reprinted from the 2002 edition

Fredonia Books
Amsterdam, The Netherlands
http://www.fredoniabooks.com

All rights reserved, including the right to reproduce this book, or portions thereof, in any form.

Foreword

When a child is abducted by a family member, the parent who has been left behind faces seemingly insurmountable obstacles. The emotional, legal, and financial difficulties precipitated by the abduction can be among the hardest challenges a parent will ever encounter. For parents whose children are taken to or retained in foreign countries, these hardships can be particularly overwhelming.

Given the complex nature of international abductions, a swift and informed response is often difficult. Unfamiliar languages and laws, compounded by the vast psychological and physical distance of the separation, can frustrate recovery efforts.

Despite these obstacles, however, it is crucial that victims of international parental kidnapping remain optimistic. Although the situation is dire, it may not be irrevocable. By responding to the abduction in a hopeful, informed, and resolute fashion, left-behind family members can marshal an effective recovery plan.

With this goal in mind, we encourage parents of abducted children to use this guidebook as a resource. It offers descriptions and realistic assessments of available civil and criminal remedies, explains applicable laws, identifies public and private resources, and identifies strategies to help left-behind parents recover their children or reestablish meaningful contact with them in another country. Our hope is that the information presented here will give parents the knowledge and support they need to reclaim their children.

Acknowledgments

The task of developing a guide for parents on the topic of international parental abduction is as complex and difficult as the subject itself. The Office of Juvenile Justice and Delinquency Prevention (OJJDP) is grateful to the many people who contributed to the development of this guide, especially parents who have experienced first hand the trauma of becoming a left-behind parent. In particular, OJJDP wishes to thank Terri Beydoun, Jodi Carlson, Jean Henderson, Tom Johnson, John LeBeau, Steve McCoy, Paul Marinkovich, Ray ("Perry") Morrison, and Jose and Miriam Santos for their commitment and contributions to the guide, and for their unfailing efforts to assist other parents who face similar circumstances.

OJJDP also wants to thank the many Federal, State, and local agencies and organizations that made significant contributions to the guide, especially: Stephanie Crews, Kevin Gutfliesh, and Grant Mendenhall from the Federal Bureau of Investigation's Crimes Against Children Unit; Marsha Gilmer-Tullis, Nancy Hammer, and John Rabun from the National Center for Missing and Exploited Children; Judy Schretter from the Child Exploitation and Obscenity Section of the U.S. Department of Justice; and Ann McGahuey and Jim Schuler from the U.S. Department of State.

Special thanks also go to the many professionals who gave their time, energy, talents, and expertise to put together a document that is effective in its delivery of information, timely in its content, and both supportive and helpful in its message to parents. This includes Helen N. Connelly, James P. Finley, and Joellen Talbot of Fox Valley Technical College; and Heather Keegan and Donna Uzell of the Florida Department of Law Enforcement.

This document would not have been possible without the invaluable assistance from Patricia Hoff, Esq., who painstakingly gave her time, talents, expertise, and knowledge to this project. Her enormous contributions to this guide are equaled by her commitment to serve and support families and children faced with international parental abductions.

Finally, sincere thanks go to Ron Laney, Director of OJJDP's Child Protection Division, who had the vision and foresight to put together a working group to begin to address issues associated with international parental abductions. Through his leadership and commitment, this guide will serve as an invaluable resource to parents and children across the world.

This guide is dedicated to all of the families and children who have been or separated from one another. It is our sincere hope that the information contained in this guide will give you the support and direction you may need in a time of crisis.

Introduction

Every year, hundreds of children in the United States are victims of international parental kidnapping—a child's wrongful removal from the United States, or wrongful retention in another country, by a parent or other family member. Parents and other family members left behind may be overwhelmed by feelings of loss, anguish, despair, and anger—as well as confusion and uncertainty about what can be done in response.

In December 1999, the Office of Juvenile Justice and Delinquency Prevention invited a small group of left-behind and searching parents to participate in a planning and development meeting. Each one had experienced first hand the heartbreak of having a child abducted to another country or wrongfully retained abroad. Some of them had recovered their children, while others had not. They willingly shared their knowledge of international parental kidnapping—gained at tremendous personal cost—to help other parents of abducted children understand what can be done to:

- Prevent an international parental kidnapping.
- Stop a kidnapping in progress.
- Locate a kidnapped or wrongfully retained child in another country.
- Bring an abductor to justice.
- Recover a kidnapped or wrongfully retained child from another country.
- Reestablish access to a child in another country.

This guide imparts the group's practical wisdom and the hope that other parents will not have to experience the confusion and discouragement these parents did when it was not clear what to do or whom to turn to when their children were kidnapped. The group offered its suggestions for preventing international kidnapping and gave detailed advice to maximize the chance that children who are kidnapped or wrongfully retained will be returned to this country.

The guide provides descriptions and realistic assessments of the civil and criminal remedies available in international parental kidnapping cases. It explains applicable laws and identifies both the public and private resources that may be called upon when an international abduction occurs or is threatened. It gives practical advice on overcoming frequently encountered obstacles so that parents can get the help they need. The guide prepares parents for the legal and emotional difficulties they may experience and shares coping and general legal strategies to help them achieve their individual goals, whether they involve recovering a child or reestablishing meaningful access to a child in another country.

Despite the difficulties that may lie ahead and the disappointment some parents may experience, it is important not to become discouraged. Stay hopeful. Do everything that can be done to prevent or to resolve an international parental kidnapping, and use every remedy available to you. This guide will help you organize your response.

How This Guide Is Organized

Each chapter begins with a brief introduction of the topics it covers, followed by a list of Frequently Asked Questions (FAQs). The answers appear in the text. The FAQ format gives readers the option of reading an entire chapter or skipping directly to a particular question. Every chapter has a list of key points at the end, with page references to the relevant text. Space is provided at the end of each chapter for personal notes.

The content of the guide is organized as follows: Chapter 1 focuses on preventing international parental kidnapping. Chapter 2 describes what can be done to stop an abduction in progress. Chapter 3 is a guide to finding an abducted child whose whereabouts are unknown. Chapter 4 examines the civil aspects of international parental kidnapping (that is, the remedies a parent may pursue to recover an abducted or wrongfully retained child). This chapter describes the Hague Convention on the Civil Aspects of International Child Abduction (called the Hague Convention), as well as legal solutions in countries not party to the Hague Convention. It lists specific countries that the United States has cited for not complying with the Hague Convention and identifies other countries with legal, social welfare, or religious systems that may prevent the return of an abducted or retained child. Chapter 5 explains the criminal aspects of international parental kidnapping (that is, the process by which the government brings abductors to justice). Chapter 6 describes other resources that may be instrumental in resolving an international parental kidnapping case, including the media, diplomatic and congressional (or other political) interventions, human rights laws and organizations, and the National Center for Missing and Exploited Children (NCMEC). Chapter 7 focuses on the legal, psychological, and practical issues surrounding a child's reunification with the left-behind parent and family. At the back of the guide are a list of recommended readings; a directory of all the resources, including Web sites, mentioned in the guide; a Hague Convention application, with instructions; a checklist for parents involved in non-Hague cases; an index containing all the questions posed in the guide; and information about the parents who contributed to the guide. Quotes from the parents appear throughout the guide.

Getting the Most From This Guide

If you are too overwhelmed now to read the guide yourself, ask family members, friends, or other support persons to read it for you. Share it with your lawyer or other advocate (for instance, a trusted friend or caseworker). The guide will be especially informative for lawyers who have limited experience in international parental kidnapping law. It will give them an overview of the remedies available to you. As you review this guide, please remember to consult with an attorney for help and assistance on any legal matters. Bring the guide to meetings with law enforcement, government personnel, and elected representatives. Lend it to journalists who are publicizing your case. Let this guide empower you to aggressively seek and obtain help in preventing or satisfactorily resolving your child's international parental kidnapping.

1. Preventing International Parental Kidnapping

This chapter describes steps parents can take to reduce the risk of international parental kidnapping. You should read this chapter if:

- *You have suspicions or evidence that the other parent is planning to take your child to another country without your permission.*
- *You are wary about letting your child visit in another country for fear the child will not be returned.*
- *You believe that "an ounce of prevention is worth a pound of cure" and want to do whatever you can to prevent an abduction or wrongful retention.*

Although no prevention measures are foolproof—some abductors will succeed even if comprehensive safeguards are in place—chances are they will deter many would-be abductors. When they do work, children are spared the harmful effects of an abduction, and parents are spared the uncertainties of seeking the return of a child from a foreign country.

Ⓠ Frequently Asked Questions

Why is it important to recognize the risk of international parental kidnapping and to put appropriate safeguards in place?

Are there warning signs that your child is at risk of international parental kidnapping?

What are the personality profiles of parents who may pose an abduction risk?

What can a court do to reduce the risk of international parental kidnapping?

How can you persuade a judge that prevention provisions are needed?

Where can you find information about the potential obstacles to recovering a child from a particular country?

If you have made the case for prevention provisions, how do you know which ones to request?

What kinds of prevention provisions can a court include in its order?

Apart from asking a judge to include prevention measures in a court order, what else can a parent do to reduce the risk of abduction?

Q: Why is it important to recognize the risk of international parental kidnapping and to put appropriate safeguards in place?

There are two reasons why parents should be alert to the possibility of abduction and take steps to prevent it. The most important reason is to protect your child from the potentially harmful effects of international kidnapping. These are described later (see "Potential harm to the child" on page 6 and "What myths hinder criminal prosecution and investigation, and how can they be dispelled?" on page 80). The second reason is to avoid the legal complications and unpredictable outcomes associated with recovery efforts in another country.

Once a child is abducted from this country to another, the laws, policies, and procedures of the foreign country determine whether and how the child will be returned. U.S. domestic law, which is favorable to recovering children who are abducted *to* this country, is not the controlling law once a child is in another country. This is true even if the abducted child is a U.S. citizen. The U.S. Government may be able to help with your case, but it does not control the outcome.

Many countries send children back to the United States under the Hague Convention on the Civil Aspects of International Child Abduction, but others have a poor record of compliance with the treaty. Some countries enforce U.S. custody and visitation orders, but many do not. Many countries allow their courts to make custody decisions concerning the child, irrespective of custody orders made in this country. These custody decisions may be based on gender or nationality rather than the child's best interests, often to the detriment of the child and the American parent. In many countries, there is a probability that return will never occur. Some countries provide for visitation for the left-behind parent but may restrict those visits to the foreign country, and such overseas visitation is not effectively enforceable except in the country that orders it. Other countries may not provide visitation at all. Many countries will not extradite their citizens for any offense, including international parental kidnapping, and several have even refused to extradite American abductors back to the United States.

You can see from the possible complications surrounding child recovery from another country why prevention efforts in this country are so important. Read on to find out when safeguards are needed and which ones may work.

Q: Are there warning signs that your child is at risk of international parental kidnapping?

Although there are no foolproof warning signs or psychological profiles for abduction risk, there are some indicators that should not be ignored. Be alert to the warning signs that an international kidnapping may be in the offing. It may be a "red flag" if a parent has:

- Previously abducted or threatened to abduct the child. Some threats are unmistakable, such as when an angry or vindictive parent verbally threatens to kidnap the child so that "you will never see the child again." Others are less direct. For instance, you may learn about the other parent's plans through casual conversation with your child.

- Citizenship in another country and strong emotional or cultural ties to the country of origin.

- Friends or family living in another country.

- No strong ties to the child's home State.

- A strong support network.

- No financial reason to stay in the area (e.g., the parent is unemployed, able to work anywhere, or is financially independent).

- Engaged in planning activities, such as quitting a job; selling a home; terminating a lease; closing a bank account or liquidating other assets; hiding or destroying documents; or securing a passport, a birth certificate, or school or medical records.

- A history of marital instability, lack of cooperation with the other parent, domestic violence, or child abuse.

- Reacted jealously to or felt threatened by the other parent's remarriage or new romantic involvement.

- A criminal record.

What are the personality profiles of parents who may pose an abduction risk?

Six personality profiles that may be helpful in predicting which parents may pose a risk of abduction are identified by Girdner and Johnston in their research report *Prevention of Family Abduction Through Early Identification of Risk Factors* (listed in the "Recommended Reading" section at the end of this guide). Keep in mind that while these profiles may be helpful in predicting which parents may pose a risk of abduction, they do not guarantee that parents who fit a particular profile will abduct or that parents who do not fit a profile will not. The six profiles are as follows:

- Profile 1: Parents who have threatened to abduct or have abducted previously.

- Profile 2: Parents who are suspicious or distrustful because of their belief that abuse has occurred and who have social support for their belief.

- Profile 3: Parents who are paranoid.

- Profile 4: Parents who are sociopathic.

- Profile 5: Parents who have strong ties to another country and are ending a mixed-culture marriage.

- Profile 6: Parents who feel disenfranchised from the legal system (e.g., those who are poor, a minority, or victims of abuse) and have family and social support.

Abducting parents across the six personality profiles share many common characteristics. They are likely to deny or dismiss the value of the other parent to the child. They believe they know what is best for the child, and they cannot see how or why they should share parenting with the other parent. They are likely to have very young children who are easy to transport and conceal and who are unlikely to protest verbally or tell others of their plight. With the exception of the paranoid profile, abducting parents are apt to have the financial and moral support of a network of family, friends, and/or cultural, community, or underground groups. Many abductors do not consider their actions illegal or morally wrong. Finally, mothers and fathers are equally likely to abduct, although at different times—fathers before a court order, mothers after an order has been made.

Parents who fit profile 5—those who are citizens of another country (or who have dual citizenship with the United States) and who also have strong ties to their extended family in their country of origin—have long been recognized as abduction risks. The risk is especially acute at the time of parental separation and divorce, when the parent feels cast adrift from a mixed-culture marriage and a need to return to ethnic or religious roots for emotional support and to reconstitute a shaken self-identity. Often, in reaction to being rendered helpless or to the insult of feeling rejected and discarded by the ex-spouse, a parent may try to take unilateral action by returning with the child to his or her family of origin. This is a way of insisting that one cultural identity be given preeminent status over the other in the child's upbringing. Often the parent will have idealized his or her own culture, childhood, and family of origin.

You can learn more about these risk profiles in several reports listed in the "Recommended Reading" section at the end of this guide.

Q What can a court do to reduce the risk of international parental kidnapping?

Ask a judge to include prevention provisions in your custody order. If you are concerned about the possibility of an abduction when you are going through divorce or custody proceedings, try to have appropriate prevention provisions included in the initial custody order.

If the initial order does not contain prevention provisions but the situation changes and you need them now, you will have to go back to court to request a modification of the original order.

You may be able to get an emergency order if time is of the essence—for instance, to stop an abductor from leaving the country with the child. Timing and good luck may work in your favor, but don't count on it! The better course is to go to court for prevention provisions before an abduction occurs. Your lawyer should review the Federal Parental Kidnapping Prevention Act (PKPA) (28 U.S.C. § 1738A) and your State's custody jurisdiction law (either the Uniform Child Custody Jurisdiction Act or the Uniform Child Custody Jurisdiction and Enforcement Act) to determine which State has jurisdiction to modify the initial order.

Q How can you persuade a judge that prevention provisions are needed?

Many judges lack experience with international parental kidnapping cases and need to be educated about the problem and what they can do to prevent it. You must go to court prepared to show the court why prevention provisions are needed. Make sure you are armed with information about the facts surrounding international parental kidnapping as well as information about your personal situation. Focus your argument on three factors: first, the risk of abduction; second, the potential harm the child is likely to suffer if abducted; and third, obstacles to locating and recovering the child if an abduction occurs. When the risk of abduction is high, when the child is likely to be harmed, and when obstacles to recovery exist that would be difficult to overcome, strict preventive measures are needed. When the risk of abduction is low, when the likelihood of recovery is high, and when little or no projected harm to the child exists, less restrictive measures should suffice.

Risk of abduction. The judge should be made aware of all the relevant red flags of a possible abduction. A list of warning signs appears on pages 4–5. Also inform the court if the other parent fits one of the six personality profiles of an abductor and thus may pose a risk for abduction. The six profiles are described on page 5.

Potential harm to the child. Parents who kidnap their children seldom have their children's best interests at heart. The experience can cause lasting psychological harm to the young victims. Some abductors live a fugitive existence, moving around and concealing their true identities to avoid detection. A child's name and appearance may be altered. A child may be kept out of school to avoid detection through school records. Abducted children may be told that they are not loved by the left-behind parent or that the searching parent is dead. They may be taught to fear the very people who could help them: police, teachers, and doctors. They may be neglected by their abductors.

In addition to causing psychological harm, some abductors pose a risk of physical harm to their children, both during and after the abduction. Parents most likely to harm their children are those who have serious mental and personality disorders, a history of violence or abuse, or little or no prior relationship with the child.

Obstacles to the location, recovery, and return of parentally abducted children. In addition to the personal issues between parents that may hinder the return of a child, obstacles can be legal, procedural, cultural, and practical, as the following examples illustrate. Lack of funds can hinder a parent's ability to hire lawyers and search for an abducted child. Law enforcement agencies may fail to take missing children's reports, to make National Crime Information Center (NCIC) entries, and to actively investigate. State and Federal statutes may provide incomplete or inadequate remedies. Foreign law may be unfriendly toward returning a child to the United States. International abductions to a non-Hague country may present insurmountable obstacles if that country does not recognize U.S. court orders, favors its own nationals, or awards custody based on religious, cultural, or gender grounds.

Abductions to most countries that are party to the Hague Convention on the Civil Aspects of International Child Abduction (described in chapter 4) present fewer obstacles because a legal remedy exists to seek the child's return. However, some countries have been cited by the U.S. Department of State for noncompliance with the Hague Convention. (See "What issues have arisen under the Hague Convention that you (and your lawyer) should know about?" on page 53) Notwithstanding the Hague Convention, prevention measures will be needed when these (and possibly other) Hague countries are involved.

Where can you find information about the potential obstacles to recovering a child from a particular country?

Try to get first-hand information from a parent who has had a child taken to or kept in the same country as your child. Review the State Department's country-specific flyers, available on the Department's Web site (www.travel.state.gov/abduct.html). You may be able to find a flyer about the country in question, but be aware that the list of flyers is incomplete, and the absence of a flyer for a particular country has no particular meaning. (See the "Directory of Resources" section of this guide for contact information.) Also, check with the embassy or consulate of the foreign country in question. If you have the resources, consider hiring an expert on foreign law to advise you and/or to testify in court. Foreign lawyers and law professors may have the expertise you need.

Judges in the United States who handle custody and divorce cases need to be informed about a foreign country's track record for returning children to the United States. They need to know if a country categorically refuses return to certain groups. This will influence how judges write their custody orders and whether they allow children to travel abroad for visits.

—Tom Johnson

Team H.O.P.E. Team H.O.P.E. (Help Offering Parents Empowerment) is a national support network that can match you with parent volunteers who have experienced an abduction in their family and who have been trained to provide support and assistance. The network was established by the Missing and Exploited Children's Program in the U.S. Department of Justice, Office of Juvenile Justice and Delinquency Prevention. Call Team H.O.P.E. (800–306–6311) and ask to speak to a parent mentor.

Department of State, Office of Children's Issues (OCI). Excellent prevention information is available online at the State Department's Web site (www.travel.state.gov). If you do not have a personal computer, it is worth going to a public library to log on to this site. Go to the site and click on "International Parental Child Abduction" for the following prevention-related information:

- Child Passport Issuance Alert Program.

- Countries that are party to the Hague Convention on the Civil Aspects of International Child Abduction.

- Country-specific abduction flyers.

- Report: From the Law Library of Congress to the Senate Foreign Relations Committee on the Operation of the Hague Convention in [25] Other Countries, October 2000.

- Reports on compliance with the Hague Convention (2001, 2000, and 1999).

- Report: Hague Convention: Applicable Law and Institutional Framework Within Certain Convention Countries.

- Congressional testimony: 10/14/99 Statement of Assistant Secretary Mary A. Ryan Before the Committee on International Relations, U.S. House of Representatives, on Implementation of the Hague Convention on the Civil Aspects of International Child Abduction.

- Islamic family law.

You can also telephone OCI for any of this information. Ask the staff if the country you are concerned about has ratified the Hague Convention and, if so, if data are available on the outcome of return applications in that country. Ask if the country has laws to enforce compliance with Hague Convention return orders. (It does little good to have a return order that cannot be enforced.) If the country is not a party to the Hague Convention, ask about its track record honoring U.S. custody decrees and helping U.S. citizens recover their children. Ask for a flyer describing custody law in the particular country. Ask OCI if there are any parents of children who have been abducted to or retained in the country in question who are willing to speak with you. Alternatively, ask OCI to give your name to such parents with a request to be contacted. OCI can also provide a list of lawyers in the foreign country whom you may consult to learn about legal obstacles you would face in seeking to recover your child.

OCI also can assist in preventing issuance of U.S. passports for children who are vulnerable to international child abduction. (See "Apart from asking a judge to include prevention measures in a court order, what else can a parent do to reduce the risk of abduction?" on page 13.)

Foreign embassy or consulate (or U.S. Embassy in the foreign country). If one of the child's parents was born in another country, contact the embassy or consulate of that country and find out about the foreign government's policies regarding parental kidnapping and child custody. (*Note:* Many countries, including some Hague countries, do not recognize parental kidnapping as a crime, making international extradition unavailable.) Also inquire if any particular prevention measures are recommended. Foreign embassies are located in Washington, DC. Many countries maintain consulates in major cities in the United States. The State Department's Web site has a list of contact information for foreign embassies in the United States. Or, check the phone book or call the operator for telephone numbers. Some foreign countries have Web sites where relevant information is posted.

A list of questions to ask is presented below. The answers may dictate the prevention measures you'll need. Not only will you know what to expect if your child is abducted to that country, but the information may persuade the court to order the prevention measures you seek. If the foreign embassy or consulate does not answer your questions, ask the U.S. Embassy located in that country. Or, if you have the financial means, you can seek answers to these questions directly from reputable lawyers in the foreign country.

Questions to ask:

- Does the foreign parent retain citizenship in his or her country of origin if he or she has become a U.S. citizen? If so, is the child automatically a citizen of that country? (The child may be a "dual national"—that is, a citizen of both the United States and another country.)

- Will the foreign government issue a passport or other travel documents to the child at the request of its national-parent? Will the foreign government issue these travel documents if courts in the United States have forbidden the child's removal from the United States? Will the foreign government notify the custodial parent if it receives an application for travel documents for the child?

- Will the foreign government or courts honor a custody order issued in the United States or otherwise assist in returning an abducted child to the United States? How can the custodial parent get a court order enforced?

- How does a parent recover a child from the country? If custody is granted, will the parent be able to take the child out of the foreign country?

- Are there any social, political, or religious attitudes or unrest in the country that could hinder efforts to recover the child?

- If the left-behind parent has visitation rights, will he or she be able to exercise them in the United States—that is, will the child be sent to the United States for visits—or will the parent have to visit the child in the foreign country?

- What are the policies of the foreign government regarding extradition? Will it extradite its own national if that person is charged in the United States with parental kidnapping? Does it make a difference if the criminal charges are State or Federal? Will the foreign government cooperate if you share custody with the other parent? Will the other parent cooperate?

National Center for Missing and Exploited Children. NCMEC also maintains information similar to that which is maintained by OCI. This includes information on prevention resources (particularly relating to non-Hague countries), and maintains statistics on cases reported to NCMEC. Call NCMEC (800–843–5678) for more information.

Q: If you have made the case for prevention provisions, how do you know which ones to request?

The sample prevention provisions listed below, and others you may think of, may be used alone or in combination. The challenge is to decide which ones are most likely to prevent the other parent from abducting or wrongfully retaining your child. Your lawyer needs your input to make appropriate choices. Describe the would-be abductor. Is he or she a citizen of another country? Does he or she have relatives living abroad? If so, in what country? What are his or her financial circumstances? What is his or her personality?

But be careful what you ask for. Too many restrictions can trigger a kidnapping. For instance, if visitation is made too infrequent or too structured, the noncustodial parent may feel that abduction is the only way to have a relationship with the child. In considering limits on the noncustodial parent's access to the child, consider your child's feelings about the noncustodial parent, which may differ markedly from your own.

Q: What kinds of prevention provisions can a court include in its order?

Listed below are sample prevention provisions you can ask a court to include in its order. Share this information with your lawyer.

Statement of the basis of the court's jurisdiction and the manner in which notice and opportunity to be heard were given. This belongs in every well-written custody order.

Specified custody and visitation rights. Clearly define the custody and visitation rights (referred to in some States as parenting responsibilities, parenting plans, or parenting time) of each party, including grandparents who have been granted visitation.

Avoid vague language such as "reasonable visitation." A parent who takes a child abroad for a "short" visit may think it reasonable to stay for 3 months, while the custodial parent may find it entirely unreasonable when the child is not back in time for school. Who is right? Resolving this question may mean more litigation. Another consequence of vague drafting is that law enforcement authorities may be reluctant to get involved. Their job is to enforce the law, not write it. One solution is to specify when visits are to start and end (i.e., dates and times), or if different terminology is used (e.g., parenting time or joint custody), when and with whom the child is to be at all times.

Statement of the penalties for violating the order on the first page of the order. Include a provision, prominently placed on the first page of the order, stating unambiguously that violation of the order may subject the violator to civil and/or criminal penalties. Ask the judge to advise the parties while they are in court about the possible consequences of noncompliance.

Supervised visitation. Unless a court suspends visits altogether, some situations warrant supervised visitation, such as when an abduction has previously occurred or abduction threats have been made, when there is evidence of domestic violence or child abuse, and when there is a possibility that the child will be abducted to or kept in a country from which recovery would be extremely difficult. Ask the judge to allow visits only at a designated place (e.g., the custodial parent's home or a supervised visitation center), at designated times, and under the supervision of a person designated by the court (such as a social worker, clergyman, or relative).

For referral to a supervised visitation center in your area, check the Web site of the Supervised Visitation Network's clearinghouse at www.svnetwork.net.

No-removal clause. Restrict the noncustodial parent's right to remove the child from the State and/or country without prior consent of the court or written consent of the custodial parent. Such a restriction enables a parent to prevent issuance of a U.S. passport for the child. (See "Apart from asking a judge to include prevention measures in a court order, what else can a parent do to reduce the risk of abduction?" on page 13.)

Caveat: This provision will not prevent issuance of a passport by another country if the child is a national of that country.

A restraining order that prohibits a potential abductor from removing a child from the country can be very helpful. Such an order was instrumental in our case. Without it, the State may not have issued a warrant at all.
—Jean Henderson

Surrender of passports and other travel documents. Require the noncustodial parent to surrender all passports—belonging to both the parent and the child—in his or her possession to a person designated by the court *before* visiting the child. But be aware that this requirement is no guarantee that the abductor will not flee with the child.

Prohibition on application for a new or replacement passport for the child. Prohibit the noncustodial parent from applying for a new or replacement passport for the child without prior written consent of the custodial parent or the court.

Caveat: Foreign governments are not bound by U.S. custody orders and may issue passports to children who are their nationals.

Notification of the foreign consulate of passport restrictions. The court may direct the foreign parent to notify his or her embassy or consulate of the order prohibiting issuance of a new or replacement passport for the child and require the parent to furnish the court with a letter from the foreign embassy or consulate acknowledging receipt of the order. Although foreign governments are under no legal mandate to do so, they may comply voluntarily with U.S. court orders.

Mirror image order. As a condition prerequisite to allowing a child to travel abroad for visits, the court may require the noncustodial parent to obtain an order from a court in the country where the visits are to occur with the same terms as the U.S. custody order.

Caveat: Although courts in a few countries (probably limited to Australia, Canada, New Zealand, and the United Kingdom) may issue identical orders without reopening the custody and visitation issues on the merits, courts in many other countries may exercise custody jurisdiction and change the underlying order or ignore provisions that conflict with their internal laws. To gauge the possible risks involved, it is a good idea to consult a knowledgeable attorney in the foreign country before asking a U.S. judge to require the other parent to obtain a mirror order.

General information on the laws of the foreign country in question may be available from the National Center for Missing and Exploited Children, the Office of Children's Issues in the U.S. Department of State, or the foreign embassy or consulate. Be aware that some countries lack the legal mechanisms to enforce even their own orders. In that circumstance, a mirror image order might not serve its intended purpose.

Assurances of return from foreign visits. In conjunction with allowing visits to occur in another country, a court may require a noncustodial parent to give assurances that the child will be returned. For instance, a court may order a noncustodial parent to provide the custodial parent with the child's travel itinerary (e.g., copies of the child's round-trip airline ticket), a list of addresses and telephone numbers where the child will be staying, and an open airline ticket for the custodial parent in case the child is not returned.

Definition of terms in the custody determination to facilitate use of the Hague Convention on the Civil Aspects of International Child Abduction. Include a provision in the custody order declaring the United States to be the child's "country of habitual residence." Although this would not bind a foreign court applying the Hague Convention, it may be persuasive. Determining the child's country of habitual residence is important for several reasons: First, the Hague Convention remedy is available only if the child is wrongfully removed from or retained outside of his or her country of habitual residence; second, the laws of the child's country of habitual residence determine whether a removal or retention is wrongful, and thus actionable, under the Hague Convention; and third, a child is normally ordered returned to the country of habitual residence.

Also include language in a U.S. custody order expressly granting you the right to determine

the child's place of residence. Again, while not binding, this may help clarify for a foreign court that you have "custody rights" within the meaning of Article 5 of the Hague Convention, and thus the right to seek the child's return.

Restrictions on the custodial parent's right to relocate with the child. A noncustodial parent may be concerned that a custodial parent's move to a foreign country may make visitation impractical (e.g., too costly or infrequent) or impossible (e.g., the foreign country may not honor an American custody/visitation order). To protect visitation rights, a noncustodial parent may seek a provision in the custody determination requiring the custodial parent to give advance notice or obtain the court's permission before relocating with the child. Some courts applying the Hague Convention have interpreted such provisions as granting custody rights, which in turn have allowed noncustodial parents to seek a child's return under the Hague Convention. This is a much more effective remedy than otherwise provided for in Article 20 of the Hague Convention when access rights are violated.

Caveat: There is a growing body of case law in the United States concerning the right of a custodial parent to relocate with the child. The trend favors allowing relocation. Noncustodial parents and their lawyers should review State law to find out what standards, tests, and/or presumptions apply in their State.

Anticipation of future moves in the custody order. Parents can avoid postjudgment litigation by anticipating future moves in the initial custody order. For instance, foreign moves may be expressly authorized, along with changes in visitation that reflect the time, distance, and expense involved in international visits. The order should also require that parents keep each other informed of new addresses and telephone numbers.

Bonds and other guarantees. When there is a risk of child abduction or noncompliance with the provisions of a custody or visitation order, ask the court to require a parent to post a bond (or give some other security or guarantee) to ensure compliance. Some States have enacted laws governing issuance of bonds in child custody cases. In other States, courts have inherent power to order a party to post a bond to protect the integrity of their orders. Information on obtaining child custody and visitation bonds is available from the Professional Bail Agents of the United States, listed in the "Directory of Resources" section of this guide.

Bond should be set in an amount sufficient to deter an abduction or wrongful removal, taking into account the financial circumstances of the obligor parent (the parent who posts the bond). A wealthy parent may be required to post a very substantial cash bond (e.g., $100,000 or more). A parent with limited resources may be ordered to post a small bond or to deposit title to real or personal property (e.g., a car) with the court in lieu of a cash bond. The property would be held in escrow pending compliance with the order (e.g., return of the child).

The obligor forfeits the bond if he or she abducts the child or otherwise violates its conditions. Upon forfeiture, the money or property should be released to the obligee (the parent whose custody or visitation rights have been violated). The obligee may have to file a motion with the court to hold the obligor parent in contempt and to order payment on the bond.

Joint custody orders. Although increasingly popular, joint custody orders should be avoided when (1) there is a history of family violence or parental kidnapping; (2) one parent opposes it; (3) there is friction between the parents; or (4) the parents live in different States or countries.

If joint custody is ordered, the custody order should be very specific about the child's residential arrangements. Specificity is particularly important for enforcement purposes. Courts need to know what they are enforcing, and law enforcement officers are reluctant to intervene in an alleged custodial interference case if the court order is vague about where and with whom the child should be.

Law enforcement assistance. Many law enforcement officers are unclear about their role in preventing and responding to parental kidnapping cases. A provision in the custody order directing law enforcement officers to take specific actions may produce faster, more effective assistance for you. One useful provision directs the police to "accompany and assist" the victim parent in recovering the child. If an abductor succeeds in removing the child from the United States, such a provision in a U.S. court order is not binding on foreign law enforcement, although it may influence their actions.

Prohibition of unauthorized pick up of the child. Prohibit the noncustodial parent from picking up the child from school, daycare centers, and babysitters, unless the custodial parent gives written permission.

Q Apart from asking a judge to include prevention measures in a court order, what else can a parent do to reduce the risk of abduction?

Ask the Office of Children's Issues in the Department of State to flag a U.S. passport application for your child and/or to deny issuance of a U.S. passport for your child. If you fear that your child may be taken abroad by the other parent without your consent, you may request that OCI enter your child's name into the Children's Passport Issuance Alert Program. Then, if a passport application for the child is received anywhere in the United States or at any U.S. Embassy or consulate abroad, you will be informed before a passport is issued for the child. You can also ask OCI to deny issuance of a passport for your child if you have a court order from a court of competent jurisdiction that either grants you sole custody or that forbids the child from traveling outside the United States without your court's consent.

Parents should be aware of a recent change in passport law that is meant to deter international parental kidnapping by limiting a parent's ability to obtain a child's passport without the other parent's knowledge and consent. The new law requires both parents to sign the passport application for a minor child under age 14. There are two exceptions: when exigent circumstances threaten the health and welfare of the child, or when the Secretary of State determines that issuance of a passport is warranted because of special family circumstances. Implementing regulations address how one parent can execute an application when the other parent is unavailable.

To inquire about a child's U.S. passport, have your child's name entered in the Children's Passport Issuance Alert Program, or to block issuance of a child's passport, you may send a written request, by mail or fax, to the Office of Children's Issues. Provide the child's full name, date and place of birth, your address, telephone number(s), and signature. If you have a custody order, send a copy. You may use the form at the end of this chapter (copies are also available from the Office of Children's Issues Web site at www.travel.state.gov).

You cannot get passport information about the other parent. But both parents may request information about their child's U.S. passport absent a court order to the contrary.

Revoking a child's U.S. passport. The longstanding policy against revoking a child's passport is being reviewed, and changes to the regulation are under advisement. (The abductor's U.S. passport is subject to revocation, or a

passport may be denied, at the request of Federal law enforcement authorities. The State Department does not discuss such actions with searching parents.)

Complications of dual nationality. A child who is a U.S. citizen may also be a citizen of another country. This may occur through the child's birth abroad, through a parent who was born outside the United States, or through a parent who is a naturalized citizen of another country. A dual national child may be eligible to hold or be included in a foreign passport in addition to holding a U.S. passport. Although the Department of State will make every effort to avoid issuing a U.S. passport if the custodial parent has provided a custody decree, the Department cannot prevent embassies and consulates of other countries from issuing passports to children who are also their nationals. However, you can request the cooperation of the foreign government if your child is a dual national. Although the foreign government is not legally required to help you (or even to comply with U.S. court orders directing or requesting it not to issue passports for the child), it may do so voluntarily.

If your child is a dual national, write to the embassy or consulate of the foreign country. Ask the foreign government not to issue a passport for your child, and request to be notified if it receives an application for a passport or visa for your child. Send a certified copy of your custody decree with your letter. Send a copy of your letter to OCI. Ask OCI to write to the foreign government in support of your request.

Take pictures of your child. Law enforcement officials report that a current, high-quality photograph of a child is the single most effective tool in finding a missing child. Take profile shots as well as front poses. Buy annual school photos of your child. Take videos.

Keep a complete written description of your child. Include hair and eye color, height, weight, date of birth, birthmarks, other unique physical attributes, and other features such as glasses, contact lenses, braces, pierced ears, and tattoos.

Record your child's Social Security number. Internal Revenue Service rules require all children older than 1 year of age to have a Social Security number if they are claimed as an exemption on their parents' tax return. Write the number down and keep it in a safe place.

Have your child fingerprinted. Most police departments provide this service at no charge. They do not keep the child's prints on file; you will be given the fingerprint card for safekeeping.

Teach your child to use the telephone. Your child needs to know how to use the telephone to call for help. Teach your child your home and work telephone numbers, including area codes. You should also show your child how to call an operator in an emergency. Tell the child you will accept collect calls. (If your workplace prohibits employees from taking collect calls, talk to the office manager about making an exception.) Reassure your child that you will always love him or her no matter what someone else may say.

Consider counseling. Counseling may help you and the other parent make smooth transitions at stressful times (e.g., the initial separation, filing of legal paperwork, issuance of final custody or divorce decrees, and the beginning of romantic relationships), which have been known to trigger abductions. Child Find of America, Inc., a nonprofit organization serving missing children and their families, offers telephone counseling for parents who are considering abducting their own children and for those who have already abducted but are now seeking to restore the child to his or her pre-abduction situation. Mediation, support services, and referrals to other organizations are also available. (Contact information for

Child Find is in the Directory of Resources section of this guide.)

Ask the police or prosecutor to intervene. If a parent (or anyone else) threatens you, your child, or another family member, do not hesitate to notify your local police department or prosecutor. Do not ignore abduction threats, especially if the parent making the threats has recently quit a job, sold a home, terminated a lease, closed a bank account, or taken any other action in preparation for flight. Such threats may indicate a growing frustration that may trigger an abduction. Ask the police or the prosecutor to inform the parent that taking a child is a crime punishable by imprisonment, fine, or both. You may be able to get a protection order under local law.

Notify schools, daycare centers, and babysitters of custody orders. Give certified copies of your custody decree to your child's school, daycare providers, and babysitters. If you fear an abduction, tell the principal and guidance counselor and ask them to alert teachers and school staff. Give them a photograph of the noncustodial parent. Ask to be alerted immediately if the noncustodial parent makes any unscheduled visits or if the child fails to arrive at school, daycare, or afterschool programs. Instruct them not to allow the child to leave the grounds without your permission.

Make a list of personal information about the other parent. Include the other parent's address, telephone number(s), Social Security or citizen identification number, driver's license number, passport number, credit cards, bank accounts, birth date, and place of birth. Gather the same information for relatives and friends—in the United States and abroad—who might help the abductor carry out an abduction. This information will not prevent an abduction, but having it can simplify efforts to locate the abductor and recover the child should an abduction occur.

Flag airline records. Contact airlines the abductor might use to leave the country and ask for their cooperation in alerting you promptly if reservations are made or tickets issued in the child's name. Consider having your lawyer contact the airlines on your behalf. If necessary, your lawyer may seek a court order to require airlines to flag records pertaining to the child.

Entry Into the Children's Passport Issuance Alert Program

REQUEST FORM. Complete one form for EACH child, and submit the completed and SIGNED request to the Office of Children's Issues by mail or fax.

1. Please provide information about each child in order to make the alert system effective. Please *print clearly or type* the information.

   Child's full name: _____

   Date of birth: _____

   Place of birth: _____

   Sex: _____

   Social Security number: _____

   U.S. passport number(s): _____

   Foreign passport number(s): _____

   List any other country(ies) involved: _____

2. Please provide the following information about yourself so that we can acknowledge your request and alert you in the future.

   Your name: _____

   Relationship to the child above: _____

   Mailing address: _____

   _____

   _____

   Telephone numbers/fax numbers: _____

   _____

3. I request that my child's name, as shown above, be entered into the Children's Passport Issuance Alert Program. Please notify me of any pending U.S. passport applications and any U.S. passports still valid for travel.

   Signed: _____ Dated: _____

   (Customary legal signature of parent or guardian)

Please read the Dual Nationality for Children information (available on OCI's Web site: www.travel.state.gov) if your child has a claim to nationality from another country in addition to U.S. citizenship.

Please mail or fax the completed, signed form(s) to the Office of Children's Issues, 2401 E Street NW, SA–1, Room L–127, Washington, DC 20037; fax: 202-663-2674. You will receive written acknowledgment and information.

Chapter One

- An ounce of prevention is worth a pound of cure.

- You may ask the court to include prevention provisions, like the ones listed in this chapter, in your initial or modification custody order. (See pages 6–7; 9–13.)

- To decide whether prevention measures are needed, evaluate three factors: first, the risk of abduction; second, the obstacles you will encounter trying to recover your child; and third, the potential harm to the child if an abduction occurs. More restrictive preventive measures will be needed when the risk of abduction is high, when the obstacles to recovering your child would be difficult to overcome, or when the abduction is likely to be particularly harmful to the child. When the risk of abduction is low and the likelihood of recovery high, less restrictive measures may be all you need.

- To assess whether there is a risk of abduction, consider whether any of the red flag warning signals described in this chapter are present and whether the would-be abductor matches any of the personality profiles described in the text. (See pages 4–5.)

- Gather information from the sources listed in this chapter to create a picture for the court about the kinds of problems you would likely encounter if you had to recover your child from another country. Use this information to craft appropriate safeguards.

- There are many things you can do without a lawyer's help to reduce the risk of abduction. They are listed in this chapter. (See pages 13–15.)

NOTES

2. Urgent Cases: Stopping an Abduction in Progress

What do you do if you discover your child has been abducted and believe the abductor is still in flight—driving toward the border, heading to an airport, traveling on an airplane bound for another country, or transiting through a foreign country en route to a final destination?

*This chapter outlines steps to take **immediately** upon making the discovery that your child has been abducted, when you believe there is still time to stop the abductor. If the abductor's scheme is discovered while he or she is still in flight, government authorities in the United States and abroad have a very narrow window of opportunity to stop the abduction. They must act swiftly and in concert. It is up to the searching parent to set the response in motion, and then to maintain close and frequent contact with relevant authorities to promote fast action.*

You must act quickly; time is of the essence. Although some abductors may not leave the country right away, law enforcement and other authorities should be alerted without delay. This at least raises the possibility of stopping the abductor and recovering the child before they leave the country or as they enter, leave, or transit another country.

Often, it is too late to stop an abduction in progress; the abductor is long gone before the searching parent discovers what has happened. Even if this describes your situation, the background information in this chapter about the Federal Bureau of Investigation (FBI), National Crime Information Center (NCIC), and INTERPOL may be of interest.

Frequently Asked Questions

Can an abductor be stopped from leaving this country?

What are the roles of the FBI, NCIC, and INTERPOL in stopping an abduction in progress and in international parental kidnapping cases generally?

Can an abductor be stopped at a foreign port of entry?

What should you do upon discovering an abduction in progress?

What is the next step if interdiction fails and the abductor succeeds?

Q: Can an abductor be stopped from leaving this country?

Yes, it is possible to stop an abduction in progress. As a general rule, law enforcement efforts to stop an abduction in progress in the United States are directed at intercepting and detaining an abductor for violating State or Federal criminal law. Unless there is a criminal warrant or facts supporting probable cause to arrest for a State or Federal criminal law violation, it is unlikely that an abduction in progress can be stopped and a child intercepted.

Caveat: You may find it difficult to get law enforcement and/or prosecutors to open an investigation, let alone charge the abductor with a criminal law violation (which you may not want to do anyway, for reasons discussed in chapter 5), in time to stop an abduction in progress.

If an abduction is not being treated as a criminal matter, it still may be possible to stop an abductor from leaving the country. If a civil court order prohibits removal of a child from the United States, a parent or law enforcement official can contact the airport authority police, who may assist in intercepting the abductor. Or, intercepting the abductor and child may depend on a chance inquiry of the NCIC Missing Person File (NCIC checks are not done routinely on travelers leaving the United States), a record on your child being in that file, and then rapid communication and coordination among law enforcement authorities to arrange for picking up the child.

Q: What are the roles of the FBI, NCIC, and INTERPOL in stopping an abduction in progress and in international parental kidnapping cases generally?

About the FBI's role in international parental kidnapping cases. The FBI has jurisdiction to investigate both interstate and international parental kidnapping cases under the Fugitive Felon Act (18 U.S.C. § 1073) and the International Parental Kidnapping Crime Act (IPKCA) (18 U.S.C. § 1204). (Both of these laws are described in chapter 5.) A parent, local law enforcement officer, or both may contact the FBI for help when an international parental kidnapping occurs.

FBI policy requires that initiation of any criminal process in international parental kidnappings be made on a case-by-case basis, in consultation with the U.S. Departments of Justice and State, the searching parent, and the affected State and Federal law enforcement agencies and prosecutors.

The FBI agent may treat an abduction in progress as a Fugitive Felon matter or a possible International Parental Kidnapping Crime Act violation and open a preliminary or full investigation. The case is investigated as any other involving a criminal fugitive who is attempting international flight. The FBI works with the lead prosecutor and local investigator.

The FBI has no investigative jurisdiction outside the United States, except on the high seas and in other locations specified by Congress. Therefore, assistance in locating missing children in other countries is limited to liaison with foreign law enforcement authorities, the FBI's Legal Attache program, and INTERPOL.

About NCIC. The FBI maintains the National Crime Information Center computer. NCIC is a computerized database available around-the-clock, every day of the year, to Federal, State, and local law enforcement authorities for criminal law enforcement purposes. Prompt NCIC entries about the child and the abductor into appropriate NCIC files improve the chances of detection in the United States.

NCIC Missing Person File (NCIC–MPF). The National Child Search Assistance Act (42 U.S.C. §§ 5779–5780) requires every Federal,

State, and local law enforcement agency to report each case of a missing child under the age of 18 to NCIC. State law enforcement agencies are prohibited from maintaining any waiting period before accepting a missing child report and are required to enter missing children reports immediately into both the State law enforcement system and the NCIC Missing Person File. *You do not need a custody order to report your child missing or for law enforcement to enter your child into NCIC–MPF. The abductor does not have to be charged with a crime.* If you have problems getting your child entered into NCIC, contact the National Center for Missing and Exploited Children (NCMEC) or your State missing children clearinghouse for assistance.

NCIC files on the abductor. The abductor may also be entered in various NCIC files, including the Vehicle File, License Plate File, the Missing Person File (in some jurisdictions), the Wanted Person File (if charged with a felony for the abduction or any other offense), and the Protection Order File. All NCIC records pertaining to the child and abductor should be cross-referenced.

NCIC entries may result in detecting the abductor or abducted child. Local, State, and Federal criminal justice agencies throughout the United States can use the NCIC computerized database to help apprehend an abductor and locate an abducted child.

If an abductor is stopped for speeding, his or her license may be run through NCIC. Any warrants in the system for the abductor will come up, and the abductor will be subject to arrest. If the NCIC record cross-references an NCIC–MPF file on the child, law enforcement authorities may detain the child temporarily pending notification to and instructions from the law enforcement office that made the missing person entry.

Although far from routine, suspicious circumstances might prompt an officer to run the child's name through NCIC. This would turn up the Missing Person File and lead to notification of the law enforcement agency seeking to locate the child.

NCIC is also accessible to Federal Inspections Service (FIS) personnel from the U.S. Customs Service and the Immigration and Naturalization Service via a computerized database called the Interagency Border Inspection System (IBIS). Although travelers departing the United States typically do not encounter exit controls (airlines, not the Federal Government, require you to present a passport), FIS personnel may conduct spot checks at U.S. borders and international airports, which could result in intercepting an abductor as he or she leaves the country. Travelers entering the United States are subject to greater scrutiny by inspection personnel. IBIS checks may detect an abductor as he or she reenters the country, with or without the child.

If, pursuant to an NCIC inquiry, an abducted child is identified at a land border, at an airport in the United States, or in a traffic stop, law enforcement authorities (e.g., the FBI, Customs/Immigration personnel, or port authority police) would temporarily detain the child and notify the originating agency that the child has been located. It is then up to that law enforcement agency to respond. Possible responses include (1) picking up the child and bringing the child before the court of jurisdiction, which would either return the child to the left-behind parent or make other placement arrangements, or (2) notifying the searching parent of the child's whereabouts and leaving recovery up to that parent. (The abductor would be subject to arrest pursuant to any outstanding criminal warrants.)

If local law enforcement fails to respond, there is still a chance the abductor could be detained if, upon further questioning by Federal authorities, it is determined that a violation of Federal criminal law (e.g., the International Parental

Kidnapping Crime Act or the Fugitive Felon Act) has occurred. Upon the abductor's arrest, the child would be turned over to appropriate State authorities. If further questioning does not support Federal criminal charges, there is no basis under Federal criminal law to continue to detain the abductor and child and they would be free to go.

About the U.S. National Central Bureau— INTERPOL. USNCB–INTERPOL serves Federal, State, and local law enforcement, as well as foreign police (*not* parents). It is accessible 24 hours per day, 7 days a week, every day of the year. USNCB can immediately contact appropriate U.S. and foreign law enforcement authorities in an effort to halt an abduction and to recover a child. Specifically, USNCB–INTERPOL can transmit messages, called "diffusions," at any time to one or any number of other national central bureaus (178 countries have national central bureaus). Diffusions can ask police authorities in those countries to search for a fugitive charged with a crime; to trace and locate an abductor, whether or not charged with a crime; and/or to locate and determine the safety and welfare of a missing or abducted child. USNCB can also communicate requests for foreign investigative assistance in abductions that have already occurred.

If an abductor and child have entered a foreign country and their location is unknown, USNCB, on behalf of U.S. law enforcement, can also request issuance of INTERPOL "color-coded notices" to search for them internationally. Red, blue, and yellow notices are issued at INTERPOL's international headquarters in France at the request of a national central bureau. The process takes at least several months.

Red notices seek persons wanted for extradition. Blue (trace and locate) notices seek persons, including abductors, whether or not they have been charged with a crime. Yellow (missing person) notices seek missing persons, including abducted children. Each notice provides all INTERPOL countries with a given person's case and identification information and asks any country locating the person to notify the requesting country immediately so that it may request extradition, facilitate a request for the child's return under the Hague Convention, or take another action, as appropriate. Foreign law enforcement agencies respond to diffusions and color-coded notices in accordance with their own laws and practices.

Can an abductor be stopped at a foreign port of entry?

There may not be enough time to organize and implement an effective interdiction effort in the United States. If the abductor escapes detection and manages to leave the United States despite urgent interdiction efforts, it may still be possible to intercept the abductor and recover the child abroad.

Successful interception abroad (i.e., stopping an abductor from entering, transiting, or leaving another country with the abducted child) depends on rapid communication and cooperation between authorities in the United States and the foreign country and a willingness on the part of authorities in that country to arrest, detain, or return the abductor or to take measures under their own law to protect the welfare of the abducted child.

The authorities in the United States likely to be involved in coordinating with foreign authorities are the FBI, USNCB–INTERPOL, the Justice Department's Office of International Affairs (OIA) and the State Department's Office of Children's Issues (OCI). The authorities in the foreign country likely to be called on are law enforcement and immigration officials and the foreign central authority for the Hague

Convention on the Civil Aspects of International Child Abduction.

If there are criminal charges. If the abductor is charged with a State or Federal crime, the State Department may submit an urgent request to the foreign government for the abductor's "provisional arrest with a view toward extradition." The FBI should also coordinate with the State Department to revoke the abductor's U.S. passport and other travel documents. If done quickly enough, the abductor would arrive in the foreign country undocumented and could be refused entry and/or ordered back to the United States.

Abductions in progress to Hague countries. If the destination country is a party to the Hague Convention on the Civil Aspects of International Child Abduction, the foreign government may be willing (though not required) to take the child into protective custody upon his or her arrival in that country if a Hague application for the child's return is filed on an urgent basis. OCI, which acts as the U.S. Central Authority for the Hague Convention, would coordinate with its counterpart central authority in the destination country.

Non-Hague countries. Authorities in countries not party to the Hague Convention may have power under their own laws to protect an abducted child even if there are no criminal charges pending against the abductor. OCI would take the lead in requesting urgent assistance to intercept a child. OCI would work with the FBI and/or local law enforcement authorities to coordinate with USNCB–INTERPOL for immediate dissemination of diffusion messages to put foreign authorities on alert for the abductor and child.

Reality check. While the U.S. Government may ask for cooperation in intercepting the abductor and victim child at a foreign port of entry, it cannot dictate how a foreign central authority or law enforcement and immigration authorities respond. The response may depend upon the nationality or gender of the abductor or child or on other intangibles over which a left-behind parent has no control, any of which may make a bid to stop an abduction in progress futile.

What should you do upon discovering an abduction in progress?

Contact government officials and organizations *without delay* to urge them to do whatever they can to stop an abduction in progress. An action checklist follows. Keep detailed records of the contacts you make.

What is the next step if interdiction fails and the abductor succeeds?

If the abductor and child take up residence in another country, the remedies available to recover your child will depend upon a combination of U.S. treaty law and the laws, case precedents, procedures, and customs of the other country. (Civil and criminal remedies for seeking return to the United States of children abducted to other countries are the topics of chapters 4 and 5.)

A Family Resource Guide on International Parental Kidnapping

Action Checklist

1. Contact local law enforcement without delay.

○ File a missing person's report on the abducted child. Ask the police to enter your child into the FBI's National Crime Information Center Missing Person File (NCIC–MPF). Provide a complete description of your child, a birth certificate, and photos. You *do not* need a custody order to have your child entered into NCIC, but bring a copy if you have one.

○ Record the name, badge number, and telephone number of the police officer who takes the missing person report. Ask for a copy. If you can't get one, ask for the case (or police report) number.

○ Verify with local law enforcement that an NCIC–MPF entry has been made. Ask for a copy of the NCIC printout. If you can't get that, ask for the NCIC record number.

Troubleshooting: Law enforcement officials may tell you that they can't do anything for 24 hours or that they can't do anything at all without a custody order. These are common mistakes! Federal law—the National Child Search Assistance Act (42 U.S.C. §§ 5779–5780)—prohibits waiting periods and does not require you to have a custody order before law enforcement enters a missing child into NCIC. Remember, if you have problems entering your child's information into NCIC, the National Center for Missing and Exploited Children or your State missing children clearinghouse may be able to help. You can also contact the local FBI Field Office (check the front of your local telephone book for the number) and request that an agent make an entry for your child in the NCIC database. The FBI has authority to do so under the Missing Children Act (28 U.S.C. § 534).

○ Ask local law enforcement to contact the FBI Field Office *as soon as possible* for immediate assistance to stop the abductor from leaving the country (or entering or exiting another). You can call the FBI directly and ask for their urgent attention to the abduction in progress. (See #3, below.)

○ Ask local law enforcement to contact the U.S. National Central Bureau–INTERPOL for immediate assistance. (See #4, below.)

○ Notify port authority police at the nearest airports, bus depots, and train stations about the abduction in progress. Fax pictures of the abductor and child.

○ Ask local law enforcement to coordinate with the prosecutor to get a local court order authorizing pick up of the child, if State law allows.

○ Find out from local law enforcement or the local prosecutor if the abductor can be criminally charged under State law. (If the destination country is a Hague Convention country with a good track record of returning children to the United States, it is important to consider

Action Checklist (continued)

whether criminal charges against the abductor might adversely affect a Hague return proceeding. This issue is discussed in chapter 5.)

○ If the abductor is charged with a State crime, ask law enforcement to make all appropriate entries in NCIC, with cross-references to the child's NCIC–MPF. If the abductor is *not* charged under State law, consult the U.S. Attorney and/or the FBI about Federal criminal charges under the International Parental Kidnapping Crime Act (described in #3, below, as well as in Chapter 4).

○ If the abductor is charged with a State felony, ask the prosecutor to request a Federal Unlawful Flight to Avoid Prosecution (UFAP) warrant. Law enforcement and prosecutors can contact the FBI or the U.S. Attorney for help in securing a UFAP warrant.

2. Report your child missing to the toll-free hotline of the National Center for Missing and Exploited Children (800–THE–LOST, or 800–843–5678).

○ Tell the operator your case is urgent.

○ Register your child with NCMEC. Your case must meet NCMEC's intake criteria for outgoing international abduction cases (i.e., children abducted from the United States or wrongfully retained abroad). NCMEC intakes outgoing cases if (1) the parent or guardian has made a police report; and (2) the parent or guardian has full or temporary custody, or the parent has filed a Hague application for the child's return, or there is a Federal warrant for the abductor under the International Parental Kidnapping Crime Act.

○ Ask to have photographs of your child and the abductor sent immediately to airports, border crossings, and other countries (if they are already out of the United States).

3. Call the closest FBI Field Office. (The telephone number is in the front of your local telephone book.)

○ Ask for immediate help to stop an abduction in progress.

○ Find out if the abductor can be charged with violating the International Parental Kidnapping Crime Act. (If the destination country is a Hague Convention country with a good track record of returning children to the United States, it is important to consider whether criminal charges against the abductor might adversely affect a Hague return proceeding. This issue is discussed in chapter 5.) If the abductor has already been criminally charged under State law, it is unlikely the Federal Government will charge the abductor with an IPKCA violation. However, it may be possible to secure a Federal UFAP warrant.

Action Checklist (continued)

○ If the FBI agent is inexperienced with parental kidnapping cases, the agent can contact the division's Crimes Against Children Coordinator or the Crimes Against Children Unit at FBI Headquarters in Washington, DC, for technical assistance. (Contact information is in the Directory of Resources section of this guide.)

4. Ask local law enforcement or the FBI to contact USNCB–INTERPOL *without delay* for assistance in stopping an international abduction in progress.

Law enforcement can contact USNCB either directly or indirectly through NCMEC (NLETS: VA007019W). NCMEC acts as liaison with USNCB–INTERPOL in cases involving missing children. *Note:* USNCB does not act upon parents' requests.

5. Call the Department of State, Office of Children's Issues (U.S. Central Authority for the Hague Convention), for help in coordinating with foreign authorities to intercept your abducted child abroad.

○ Ask OCI to request that the foreign government intercept the child upon his or her arrival in that country with the abductor.

○ Find out if the Hague Convention remedy is available in your case. A list of countries party to the Hague Convention is available online at the State Department's Web site, along with the date the Convention came into force. (Abductions or wrongful retentions occurring before the Convention came into force may not be covered.) You can also check the Web site for the Hague Conference on Private International Law (www.hcch.net).

○ Ask if you should file a Hague application on an urgent basis. If so, ask how to do this and where you can get help. (A blank application and instructions are included at the back of this guide.)

○ If the destination country is not a party to the Hague Convention, ask OCI what can be done on an urgent basis to intercept the child.

○ Ask to have your child entered into the Children's Passport Issuance Alert Program. Find out if a passport has been issued to your child. If you have custody, put a hold on issuance of a U.S. passport. (See chapter 1 for more information on preventing issuance of a U.S. passport for your child.)

Action Checklist (continued)

- Ask if the abductor's U.S. passport has been revoked. Because this information is protected by the Privacy Act, you may not be given the answer. (*Note:* Although current policy does not allow a child's passport to be revoked, the policy is being reviewed, and changes to the regulation are under advisement.) Ask if the child's passport has been or could be revoked. This could be particularly helpful if the child is taken to a non-Hague country.

- If you do not already have a passport, apply for one now in case you need to travel abroad.

6. Contact airlines the abductor would be likely to fly.

- Explain the urgency of the situation. Ask if the airline has issued tickets or has booked reservations for the abductor and child. If the airline volunteers any pertinent information about the abductor's flight plans, notify law enforcement at once! Law enforcement may be able to get this information if you can't.

7. Contact the embassy or consulate of the destination country. (Telephone numbers are available online at the State Department's Web site. You can also check the local phone directory or call operator assistance.)

- Tell embassy personnel the situation and ask if they can help.

- If the abductor is a national of that country, ask if the abductor's passport can be revoked. Can this person help you do this?

8. Contact Canadian authorities if the abductor is likely to go to or through Canada.

- Contact the Royal Canadian Mounted Police Missing Children's Registry immediately if you think the abductor is going to go to or through Canada. (See the "Directory of Resources" section of this guide for contact information.) Canada has a very effective border alert system.

9. Contact Team H.O.P.E.

- Ask for a referral to a parent who has faced a similar urgent situation involving the same country. Try to get suggestions from that parent about what to do.

- It is very difficult to stop an abduction in progress. Often, it is too late; the abductor is long gone before the searching parent discovers what has happened. If the abductor's scheme is discovered while he or she is still in flight, government authorities in the United States and abroad have a narrow window of opportunity to stop the abduction. They must act swiftly and in concert. It is up to the searching parent to set the response in motion. Refer to the checklist (on page 24) for detailed advice on whom to contact and what to request.

- Contact local law enforcement without delay. Report your child missing and request immediate entry into NCIC–MPF. Request coordination with the FBI and USNCB–INTERPOL. Alert port authority police. (See pages 24–27.)

- Report your child missing to the toll-free hotline of the National Center for Missing and Exploited Children. (See page 25.)

- Call the closest FBI Field Office to request an immediate investigation. (The telephone number should be in the front of your local telephone book.) (See page 25.)

- Ask local law enforcement and the FBI to contact USNCB–INTERPOL *without delay* for immediate dissemination of diffusion messages to put law enforcement worldwide on the alert for the abductor and child and to request help stopping the abduction. (See page 26.)

- Call the Department of State, Office of Children's Issues (U.S. Central Authority for the Hague Convention), for help in coordinating with foreign authorities to intercept your abducted child abroad. (See page 26.)

- Contact airlines the abductor might use. (See page 27.)

- Contact the embassy or consulate of the destination country. (See page 27.)

NOTES

Chapter Two

3. Searching for Your Child

How do you find a child who has been abducted to or wrongfully retained in another country? If you do not know the whereabouts of your abducted child, this chapter will help you organize an international search. Use it to galvanize public and private resources to locate your child in another country. If you know your child's whereabouts, skip to the next chapter.

Frequently Asked Questions

Where can you get help finding your child?

What legal consequences might you face if you don't find your child quickly?

How long should you keep searching?

Where can you get help finding your child?

Help is available from many of the same sources that you would contact to stop an abduction in progress. That is why the action checklist in this chapter contains many of the same resources listed in chapter 2, although the focus is on location rather than interdiction. Background information on the Federal Bureau of Investigation (FBI), National Crime Information Center (NCIC), and U.S. National Central Bureau–INTERPOL (USNCB–INTERPOL) also appears in chapter 2.

> Don't let feelings of anger, grief, denial, or fear paralyze you into inaction. Let your love for your child, and your concern for your child's best interests, be your constant motivator.
> —Paul Marinkovich

What legal consequences might you face if you don't find your child quickly?

It is important to act quickly, as time can work to the abductor's legal advantage. Courts in countries that are party to the Hague Convention on the Civil Aspects of International Child Abduction (discussed in chapter 4) are not required to order a child returned if proceedings are commenced a year or more after the abduction or retention and the child has become settled in a new environment. Even if the child is ordered returned, courts in the child's country of habitual residence may be hesitant to separate the child from the abductor if strong bonds have developed between them. If the abductor has enough time to get a custody order in the destination country—Hague or non-Hague—your recovery efforts may be complicated, although not necessarily frustrated.

> Get information about the laws and procedures of the country your child has been taken to or kept in. Talk to other parents who have been in your shoes. Call Team H.O.P.E. for a referral.
> —Steve McCoy

Q How long should you keep searching?

If efforts to locate your child do not succeed at first, don't give up. Instead, remain calm and persistent. Check with all of your sources periodically, and keep a record of your contacts. Don't take your frustrations out on public officials, who may be able to help you. Other family members, friends, and missing children organization personnel are safer places to vent your emotions. Remember that most parents eventually find their abducted children, although some do so sooner than others. But even if your search seems endless, don't lose hope! Someday you may get just the tip you have been waiting for.

Your search can be very time-consuming, but try to go about your normal routines, too. You probably need to continue working, and you may have other family members who need your support and attention. And don't neglect yourself! If you need support, keep in mind that NCMEC provides information on psychologists and mental health professionals across the nation who are familiar with the issues faced by left-behind parents.

When you find your child, notify every individual, law enforcement officer, organization, government office, and media contact you have sought help from that you have recovered your child. Thank them, as appropriate, for their interest and assistance.

Action Checklist

1. If you do not know your child's whereabouts, promptly report your child missing to the local police and ask the police to enter your child into the National Crime Information Center Missing Person File (NCIC–MPF).

The statutory authority for making the entry is the Missing Children Act (28 U.S.C. § 534). The National Child Search Assistance Act (42 U.S.C. §§ 5779–5780) forbids all law enforcement agencies from establishing a waiting period before accepting a missing child report. Provide a complete description of your child, a birth certificate, and photos, if available. You do *not* need a custody order to have your child entered in NCIC, but bring a copy if you have one.

- ○ Record the name, badge number, and telephone number of the police officer who takes the missing person report. Ask for a copy. If you can't get one, ask for the case (or police report) number.

- ○ Verify with local law enforcement that an NCIC–MPF entry has been made. Ask for a copy of the NCIC printout, or try to get the NCIC record number, at least.

Troubleshooting: Law enforcement may tell you that they can't do anything for 24 hours or that they can't do anything at all without a custody order. These are common misconceptions! Federal law—the National Child Search Assistance Act—prohibits waiting periods and does not require you to have a custody order before law enforcement enters a missing child into NCIC.

- ○ Call the National Center for Missing and Exploited Children (NCMEC) *without delay*. NCMEC can confirm (but not make) entries. If the entry has not been made, ask NCMEC to contact local law enforcement about the case. Your State missing children clearinghouse may also contact law enforcement at your request. You can also contact the local FBI Field Office (check the front of your local telephone book for the number) and request that an agent enter your child into NCIC. The FBI has authority to make the entry under the Missing Children Act.

- ○ Once your child's description is entered in NCIC–MPF, ask the police to pursue a missing person investigation to locate your child. The Missing Children's Assistance Act [42 U.S.C. § 5780(3)(B)] requires law enforcement agencies that enter missing child reports into NCIC to "institute or assist with appropriate search and investigative procedures" and to maintain close liaison with NCMEC while working missing children cases.

Tell the officer about resources that can help with the investigation. For instance, law enforcement officers are "authorized persons" under the Parental Kidnapping Prevention Act who may request address information about the child and the abductor from the Federal Parent Locator Service. Mention your State missing children clearinghouse to the investigating officer, who may not be familiar with it. The clearinghouse may be able to assist with missing children investigations. (Telephone numbers for the State missing children clearinghouses are available from

Action Checklist (continued)

NCMEC.) Have the officer call NCMEC for a free copy of the law enforcement guide *Missing and Abducted Children: A Law Enforcement Guide to Case Investigation and Program Management*. Another free manual for law enforcement, *International Parental Kidnapping: A Law Enforcement Guide*, is available from the Office of Juvenile Justice and Delinquency Prevention, through the Juvenile Justice Clearinghouse (www.puborder.ncjrs.org).

○ Urge local law enforcement to contact the U.S. National Central Bureau–INTERPOL to put law enforcement in the United States and abroad on the alert for the abductor and child. (Contact information is in the Directory of Resources section of this guide.) NCMEC acts as liaison with INTERPOL for missing children cases.

2. As soon as you have reported your child missing to local law enforcement, call the National Center for Missing and Exploited Children to report the abduction and ask for help in finding your child.

○ Register your child with NCMEC. (NCMEC's intake criteria for outgoing international abduction cases are discussed on page 25.)

○ Ask NCMEC to disseminate photographs of your child and the abductor to other countries and to include your child's photo on NCMEC's Web site. (Your request will have to meet NCMEC's criteria for photo dissemination.)

○ Inquire about having your child's name included in a Voice of America alert. NCMEC helps supply this worldwide radio network with appropriate cases for multicountry broadcast.

○ Request a free copy of NCMEC's publication, *Family Abduction: How To Prevent an Abduction and What To Do If Your Child Is Abducted*. (This is also available on NCMEC's Web site, www.missingkids.com.) Chapter 4 of this guide lists many sources of information that can help you find your child. You can use the "Abduction Checklist for Parents" at the end of the guide to help you organize your search efforts.

3. Contact the Department of State, Office of Children's Issues (OCI), for help.

○ Ask for confirmation of entry into another country.

○ Ask to have your child's name entered into the Children's Passport Issuance Alert Program. Information in the passport name check system may help locate your child. (Information about the passport name check system appears in chapter 1.)

○ If your child is a U.S. citizen or a dual national, contact OCI regarding a "welfare and whereabouts" visit. If you have an open case with OCI, then mail or fax a letter to the office.

Action Checklist (continued)

Include the following information: (1) the child's full name (and any aliases); date and place of birth; passport number and date and place of issuance; and copies of any court orders or police reports; and (2) the abductor's full name (and any aliases); date and place of birth, passport number, date and place of issuance, and occupation; probable date of departure; flight information; and details of ties to a foreign country, such as the names, addresses, and telephone numbers of friends, relatives, place of employment, and business connections there. If you have photographs of the abductor and child, enclose them with your letter. You can use the checklist at the back of this guide to organize the information.

What is a "welfare and whereabouts" visit? Working with the information you provide, a U.S. consular officer overseas will try to confirm the location of your child, arrange a visit, and report back to you on your child's condition. The U.S. Embassy works with local authorities to locate the child. For example, the Diplomatic Security Service-Regional Security Officer at the U.S. Embassy abroad may call upon foreign police to help determine the child's whereabouts and/or a consular officer may request information from local officials on your child's entry or residence in the country. Unfortunately, not every country maintains such records in retrievable form, and some countries may not release such information to U.S. officials. (Searching parents should be aware that some countries may actually withhold address information when the abductor or abducted child is a citizen of the country.)

Once the child is located, a U.S. consular official will attempt to visit. If the abductor refuses, the U.S. Embassy or consulate can request assistance from local authorities, either to arrange a visit or actually conduct the visit. Following the visit, you receive a report on the child's health and welfare. It may contain your child's address in the foreign country.

Troubleshooting: In some cases, the abductor may allow a "welfare and whereabouts" visit on the condition that the child's foreign address not be disclosed. There may be ways to discover your child's address even if this happens. Ask the State Department for assistance in releasing your child's address on the grounds that the child is a U.S. citizen and you are the child's parent. (A custody order awarding you custody would probably strengthen your case.) Not only do you have a right to know where your child is, but you need to know in order to take action to recover the child. Hopefully, you will not have to resort to litigation to discover your child's address because it is expensive, time-consuming, and the results are not assured.

4. Contact the nearest FBI Field Office and ask for an investigation. (The telephone number should be in the front of your local telephone book.)

FBI policy requires that initiation of any criminal process in an international parental kidnapping be made on a case-by-case basis. The FBI agent may treat an abduction as a Fugitive Felon matter (interstate flight to avoid prosecution of a State felony crime) or as a felony under the International Parental Kidnapping Crime Act and open a preliminary or full investigation. Because the

Action Checklist (continued)

FBI has no investigative jurisdiction outside the United States, assistance in locating missing children in other countries is limited to liaison with foreign law enforcement authorities, the FBI's Legal Attache program, and INTERPOL. Any criminal investigation is centered on the abductor. If the child is located in the course of the investigation, the agent may notify the searching parent so that the parent can take steps to recover the child.

Troubleshooting: If the local FBI Field Office is reluctant to get involved (which may be due to inexperience with international abduction cases), suggest that the agent in charge contact the Office of Crimes Against Children in FBI Headquarters in Washington, DC, for technical assistance.

5. Meet with the local prosecutor to discuss the possibility of charging the abductor with a State law violation. Be sure to discuss any countervailing considerations, such as whether filing criminal charges against the abductor might adversely affect a Hague return proceeding and actually hinder the child's return. (See chapters 4 and 5.)

- If the abductor is charged with a State felony, ask the prosecutor to request a Federal Unlawful Flight to Avoid Prosecution (UFAP) warrant (18 U.S.C. § 1073). Issuance of a UFAP warrant brings the FBI into the investigation. This may improve the chances of locating the abductor and incidentally recovering the child.

6. If you think the abductor is in Canada, contact the Royal Canadian Mounted Police Missing Children's Registry. (Contact information is in the "Directory of Resources" section of this guide.)

7. While government authorities are working on your case, you should be doing some investigative work on your own.

Many of the information sources described in NCMEC's *Family Abduction* book (see #2, above) may be helpful when your child is missing in another country. A few are described in the following paragraphs.

- Flag school, birth, and medical records. Write to your child's schools and medical providers (doctors, dentists, hospitals, and pharmacies) and ask to be notified if they receive a request for your child's records. By tracing the source of the request, you may be able to narrow the search for your child to a particular area. With regard to school records, Federal law—the Family Education Rights and Privacy Act (20 U.S.C. § 1232g)—gives parents the right to find out from school officials whether their child's school records have been transferred to another school or if copies have been sent to the other parent and to learn where the records have been sent. Once that is known, the school must disclose the child's current address.

Action Checklist (continued)

- Write to the State government office that maintains birth certificates (e.g., the Bureau of Vital Statistics) and ask to be notified if the agency receives a request for your child's birth certificate. Depending on the flagging laws and policies in your area, the agency may notify you or law enforcement if it receives such a request. (In some States, law enforcement may have to request the flag.) The requesting party's return address may lead you to your child.

- Talk to friends and relatives of the abductor who may have information about your child's location and who may be sympathetic to your plight. You can convey your hurt, frustration, confusion, and sense of betrayal, but don't be confrontational or threatening. You certainly don't want to provoke the abductor into deeper hiding as a result of your overtures, but be careful not to create the impression that you accept what the abductor has done. Express your appreciation for any information they can give you.

- Contact nonprofit missing children organizations and your State missing children clearinghouse for advice and assistance. A list of State missing children clearinghouses is available from NCMEC. You can get referrals to parental kidnapping and missing children organizations from the Association of Missing and Exploited Children's Organizations. AMECO can identify organizations that have experience with international parental kidnapping and direct you to books, guides, and other resources that are available through its member organizations.

- Check (or remind authorities to check) for address information or other leads in government databases (e.g., the Federal Parent Locator Service and the Worldwide Locator Services for each branch of the military).

  Information about the Federal Parent Locator Service is available from the Office of Child Support Enforcement (contact information is in the Directory of Resources). Only "authorized persons" enumerated in Federal law (42 U.S.C. § 663) can request address information. *Parents are not authorized*. General information and requirements for using the Military Worldwide Locator Services to obtain address information for active-duty personnel and reservists are available on the Internet at www.defenselink.mil/faq/pis/PC04MLTR.html.

- Try to get telephone and financial records that might lead you to the abductor. If you can't get information voluntarily, law enforcement may obtain it in the course of a criminal investigation, or your lawyer may seek a subpoena.

- Seek publicity through both television and print media. Attempt to get pictures of your child published internationally. Talk to law enforcement first to be sure that the publicity will not adversely affect a criminal investigation.

Action Checklist (continued)

○ Consider the pros and cons of hiring a private investigator. (These are discussed in detail in NCMEC's *Family Abduction* book). Talk to other parents. Try to get recommendations from trusted sources. If you plan to hire an investigator, consider having your lawyer review the contract before you sign it. (Some parents have complained about contracts with no fee limits or protections against unauthorized add-on fees.) If you decide to hire a private investigator, keep government authorities informed of your actions and progress.

○ Check the Internet for address information, including the following search engines:

www.anywho.com
www.infospace.com
www.infousa.com
www.switchboard.com
www.whowhere.com
www.555-1212.com

8. Call Team H.O.P.E. Ask to be matched with a parent whose child has been abducted to the same country as yours. Find out how that parent went about finding his or her child.

9. If you suspect your child is in a particular country, contact the foreign embassy of that country. Ask for advice on what the foreign government can do to help and what you may be able to do on your own to find your child in that country. Ask for referrals to missing children group(s) or other agencies that serve parents of abducted children in the country.

The sources listed below may help you find your child. Refer to the text for detailed advice about how they can help.

- Local police. (See page 33.)
- National Center for Missing and Exploited Children. (See page 34.)
- Department of State, Office of Children's Issues. (See page 34.)
- Federal Bureau of Investigation. (See page 35.)
- Local prosecutor. (See page 36.)
- Foreign embassy or consulate.
- Royal Canadian Mounted Police Missing Children's Registry.
- Team H.O.P.E.
- NCMEC's book, *Family Abduction: How To Prevent an Abduction and What To Do if Your Child Is Abducted*.

Follow up on everything that has been done and share any new leads with the offices that are working with the case.

NOTES

4. Civil Remedies in International Parental Kidnapping Cases

Chapter Four

How do you go about recovering your child from another country? If there is any chance of meaningful communication with the abductor, you might try working out an agreement for your child's return. If voluntary return is not feasible and your child has been abducted to or wrongfully retained in a country that is party to the Hague Convention on the Civil Aspects of International Child Abduction, you can invoke the Hague Convention to seek the child's prompt return or use any other remedy available in that country. If your child is located in a country that is not party to the Hague Convention, then the Hague Convention is not an option, and you must seek return under other laws and procedures in effect in that country. Some countries are more likely to return children to the United States than others.

Criminal charges against the abductor may impact on your legal efforts to recover the child. They may help or hurt, depending upon the country involved and the facts of the case. In most situations where the Hague Convention is applicable, you should first try to use the Hague Convention if voluntary return is not possible and refrain from pursuing criminal remedies as long as the Hague process is under way and there appears to be a reasonable chance of success. Criminal remedies are discussed in chapter 5.

This chapter covers the following topics:

- *Voluntary return, the best possible outcome.*

- *The Hague Convention remedy: what it is, how it works, what its strengths and shortcomings are, and how criminal proceedings against the abductor may impact a return proceeding.*

- *Civil legal actions you can pursue in countries not party to the Hague Convention (and in Hague Convention countries, if you choose) that are aimed at child recovery.*

- *What to expect if a foreign court denies return of your child under the Hague Convention or other law and instead exercises custody jurisdiction.*

- *Lawsuits that can be brought in the United States against the abductor and accomplices for money damages, which may incidentally result in your child's return.*

- *Information to help you find an attorney with appropriate experience.*

Frequently Asked Questions

Voluntary Return

Is voluntary return feasible?

Where can you get help to negotiate a voluntary return?

If the abductor agrees to return the child, what can the U.S. Embassy do to facilitate the return?

What are your options if voluntary return isn't possible?

The Hague Convention on the Civil Aspects of International Child Abduction (Hague Convention)

What is the Hague Convention on the Civil Aspects of International Child Abduction?

Does the Hague Convention address visitation rights?

When did the Hague Convention take effect in the United States?

What is the International Child Abduction Remedies Act (ICARA)?

What countries are treaty partners of the United States?

What is the Hague Convention's return remedy?

When are removals or retentions "wrongful" under the Hague Convention?

Do you need a custody order to seek a child's return under the Hague Convention?

Are there any exceptions to the return obligation?

Is there an official government office responsible for administering the Hague Convention?

What assistance does the U.S. Central Authority provide?

How do you start a return action under the Hague Convention?

Do you need an attorney to bring a Hague action?

Where can you get a return application, and is help available to fill it out?

When should you start a return action?

Does the application have to be translated?

If you seek return under the Hague Convention, can you continue trying to work out a voluntary return?

Can criminal charges against an abductor impact a Hague proceeding for the child's return?

How can you find out if criminal charges will help or hurt a Hague case in a particular country?

What issues have arisen under the Hague Convention that you (and your lawyer) should know about?

Must you use the Hague Convention to seek your child's return?

What happens if a foreign court denies return of your child under the Hague Convention?

Legal Solutions in Countries Not Party to the Hague Convention (and in Hague Countries, if You Do Not Invoke the Hague Convention or Return Is Denied)

How can you find out what to do if your child is abducted to a non-Hague country?

Can the U.S. Embassy represent you in legal proceedings in the foreign country?

What can the Office of Children's Issues (OCI) in Washington and the U.S. Embassy abroad do to help?

Will a foreign court enforce a U.S. custody/visitation order?

What recourse do you have if a foreign court refuses to enforce your custody/visitation order?

What if you don't have a custody order?

Foreign Custody Jurisdiction

Under what circumstances will you have to litigate custody or visitation in the courts of a foreign country?

What are the consequences of a foreign court exercising jurisdiction?

Will you get a fair hearing?

Will you face discrimination based on gender or nationality?

Will your child's wishes be considered?

If you are awarded custody or visitation, will the order be enforceable?

Who pays?

Do you jeopardize your legal position in the United States by pursuing custody or visitation in a foreign court?

Can criminal charges in the United States against the abductor be helpful if civil proceedings abroad are not?

Children Abducted to Overseas U.S. Military Installations

Are there any special remedies if the abductor is stationed overseas with the U.S. military?

Finding a Lawyer

Do you need a lawyer?

What should you look for in a lawyer?

Where can you get referrals to lawyers who have handled international parental kidnapping cases?

What if you can't afford a lawyer?

What questions should you ask before hiring a lawyer?

What should you do if your lawyer isn't getting results?

Child-Snatching Tort Suits

What are child-snatching tort suits?

What kind of lawyer do you need for a child-snatching tort suit?

Are child-snatching tort suits advisable in every case?

The Self-Help Dilemma

Do you have to use the foreign legal system, or can you personally get your child?

Can you be prosecuted abroad?

Will your child be safe upon return to the United States?

What are the risks of hiring someone to recover your child?

Voluntary Return

 Is voluntary return feasible?

Many searching parents can skip the discussion of voluntary return because they know it is completely out of the question in their cases. But if there is even a remote chance that the abductor might reconsider his or her actions and return the child, it may be worth a shot. Your child—and your wallet—may be better off if you can resolve the case amicably without going to court. However, if you cannot negotiate with the abductor on an even playing field, you are probably better off not trying. Victims of domestic violence often fall into this category.

Caveats: You can file a Hague application while in negotiations with the other parent. However, if you negotiate with the abductor for your child's return, be careful not to say or do anything that could be interpreted as your acquiescing or consenting to the wrongful removal or retention. Acquiescence and consent are defenses to a return under the Hague Convention, which you may have to use if negotiations fail. Also bear in mind that there may be no practical way to enforce a settlement agreement if the country in question lacks enforcement procedures, which many do.

Q: Where can you get help to negotiate a voluntary return?

Help may be available from the following sources (contact information for agencies and organizations is in the Directory of Resources section of this guide):

- Friends and relatives.

- Law enforcement officials and prosecutors.

- U.S. Department of State, Office of Children's Issues (OCI), which serves as the U.S. Central Authority for the Hague Convention.

- National Center for Missing and Exploited Children (NCMEC).

- Child Find of America, Inc.

- Immigration and Naturalization Service (INS).

Friends and relatives. The abductor's friends and relatives may help you establish communication with the abductor and help mediate a solution. Their efforts could eventually result in the child's return or at least improve your chances of visiting your child and participating in his or her upbringing.

Law enforcement officials and prosecutors. Criminal justice professionals involved in the criminal aspects of the abduction may negotiate with the abductor to resolve the case. The child's return may be a condition of resolving the criminal charges. The prosecutor has exclusive say over whether criminal charges will be dismissed.

OCI and NCMEC. The Office of Children's Issues and the National Center for Missing and Exploited Children may facilitate negotiations between the left-behind parent and the abductor and help make arrangements for the child's return if negotiations succeed. If your child is in a Hague country, you can ask the U.S. Central Authority and/or the foreign central authority to help work out a voluntary resolution. The Hague Convention requires each country party to the Hague Convention to establish a central authority to carry out enumerated responsibilities, including taking appropriate measures, directly or indirectly, "to secure the voluntary return of the child or to bring about an amicable resolution of the issues." When central authorities act, they do so as facilitators, not as your legal representative. Parents should be aware that central authorities do not follow uniform practices, and the range of assistance available to American parents depends upon the particular country involved.

Child Find of America, Inc. Child Find offers professional mediation services to help resolve parental kidnapping cases. *Pro bono* (no fee) mediators act as go-betweens for the abductor and the left-behind parent in an effort to work out their differences and secure the child's return. Both parents must agree to mediate. Mediation services are available free of charge via Child Find's toll-free telephone number (800–A–WAY–OUT). Telephone mediation may be effective when face-to-face mediation is impractical. If criminal warrants are outstanding, court and law enforcement officials are informed of the mediation, the goals of the program, and the name and address of the mediator. Courts and law enforcement agencies have generally been willing to let parents work things out through the mediation process, although they are neither bound by the process nor required to drop criminal charges.

Immigration and Naturalization Service. Under 8 U.S.C. § 1182(a)(10)(C), an alien may be denied a visa or admission into the United States if he or she detains, retains, or otherwise withholds custody of a U.S. citizen child

outside of the United States in violation of a U.S. court order granting custody to the other parent, provided the child is being held in a non-Hague country and the child is unmarried and under the age of 21. Aliens who have assisted or provided material support to a child abductor may also be denied a visa or admission into the United States.

- INS, which has jurisdiction over aliens who are in or are seeking admission to the United States, can use this law to deny admission or to deport.

- State Department consular officers abroad can use this law to deny or revoke visas of aliens falling within the statute, thus preventing travel to the United States.

- Although the State Department can revoke the visa of an alien in the United States, revocation of a visa does not affect the alien's length of stay after entry or the right to stay. Therefore, revoking the visa will not terminate the alien's legal status in the United States or compel his or her departure. Revocation will, however, prevent an alien from reentering, if the alien chooses to depart voluntarily. Abductors and assisters already in the United States should be brought to the attention of INS, which has exclusive jurisdiction over aliens in the United States.

The law is a potentially powerful tool to use against an abductor or accomplice who needs to come to the United States to tend to business or family matters. The child's return becomes a precondition for entering the country.

If the abductor agrees to return the child, what can the U.S. Embassy do to facilitate the return?

If a U.S. citizen parent successfully negotiates the release of a child and obtains physical custody of the child from the abductor, and if there is no court order prohibiting the parent from removing the child from the foreign country, the U.S. Embassy or consulate in that country can provide passports and assist in obtaining exit permits. Under certain circumstances, U.S. Embassies and consulates can arrange repatriation loans to pay for the child's trip back to the United States. Financial assistance for transportation may also be available from NCMEC. Contact NCMEC or OCI for more information.

Parents should keep in touch with the State Department throughout the process. Don't wait until the last minute to get the Department involved.

What are your options if voluntary return isn't possible?

If voluntary return is not possible, parents searching for children abducted to or wrongfully retained in other countries must seek recovery under the laws in effect in that country.

Legally, U.S. consular officers must act in accordance with the laws of the country to which they are accredited. They cannot take possession of a child abducted by a parent. They are unable to assist a parent who is a U.S. citizen and is attempting a resnatch or to aid a parent attempting to act in violation of the laws of the host country. Remember that many countries do not recognize child abduction as a crime.

The Hague Convention on the Civil Aspects of International Child Abduction (Hague Convention)

Q: What is the Hague Convention on the Civil Aspects of International Child Abduction?

The Hague Convention is an international treaty that provides for the prompt return of wrongfully removed or retained children. The Hague Convention's premise is that custody of an abducted child should be decided by courts in the child's country of habitual residence and not by the abductor's unilateral actions or by courts in the country chosen by the abductor.

Q: Does the Hague Convention address visitation rights?

Yes. One of the Hague Convention's stated objectives is to secure protection for "rights of access," which, in U.S. terms, is equivalent to visitation. However, the Hague Convention *provides only limited relief* in access cases and *does not include the right of return*. Specifically, Article 21 provides that legal action may be taken "with the view to organizing or protecting these rights and securing respect for the conditions to which the exercise of these rights may be subject." Central authorities are directed to cooperate to promote the peaceful enjoyment of access rights and the fulfillment of any conditions to which they are subject. Article 21 is largely without teeth and in practice has not guaranteed that visitation rights will be honored.

Q: When did the Hague Convention take effect in the United States?

The Hague Convention took effect in the United States in 1988, following ratification and enactment of the International Child Abduction Remedies Act (42 U.S.C. §§ 11601–11610).

Q: What is the International Child Abduction Remedies Act (ICARA)?

ICARA is a Federal statute that establishes procedures for using the Hague Convention in the United States. ICARA governs proceedings brought in the United States for the return of children who have been abducted to or wrongfully retained in this country in violation of the Hague Convention. These are called *incoming* cases. *Outgoing* cases involve children wrongfully removed from the United States and taken to or wrongfully retained in a foreign country. If you are reading this because your child is wrongfully in another country, yours is an outgoing case. You must follow the procedures established by the country in which your child is located—not ICARA—to invoke the Hague Convention there.

Q: What countries are treaty partners of the United States?

Searching parents in the United States can invoke the Hague Convention only if it is in force between the United States (as the child's country of habitual residence) and the country where the child is located and if it was in force at the time of the wrongful removal or retention. As of February 2001, the Hague Convention was in force between the United States and the following nations. The date the Convention took effect is indicated in parentheses:

Argentina (6/1/91)
Australia (7/1/88)
Austria (10/1/88)
Bahamas (1/1/94)

Belgium (5/1/99)
Belize (11/1/89)
Bosnia and Herzegovina (12/1/91)
Burkino Faso (1/1/92)
Canada (7/1/88)
Chile (7/1/94)
China
   Hong Kong Special Administrative Region 1 (9/1/97)
   Macau (3/1/99)
Colombia (6/1/99)
Croatia (12/1/91)
Cyprus (3/1/95)
Czech Republic (3/1/98)
Denmark (except the Faroe Islands and Greenland) (7/1/92)
Ecuador (4/1/92)
Finland (8/1/94)
France (7/1/98)
Germany (12/1/90)
Greece (12/1/90)
Honduras (6/1/94)
Hungary (7/1/88)
Iceland (12/1/96)
Ireland (10/1/91)
Israel (12/1/91)
Italy (5/1/95)
Luxembourg (7/1/88)
Former Yugoslav Republic of Macedonia (12/1/91)
Mauritius (10/1/93)
Mexico (10/1/91)
Monaco (6/1/93)
Netherlands (9/1/90)
New Zealand (10/1/91)
Norway (4/1/89)
Panama (6/1/94)
Poland (11/1/92)
Portugal (7/1/88)
Romania (6/1/93)
Slovak Republic (2/1/01)
Slovenia (4/1/95)
South Africa (11/1/97)
Spain (7/1/88)
St. Kitts and Nevis (6/1/95)
Sweden (6/1/89)
Switzerland (7/1/88)
Turkey (8/1/00)
United Kingdom of Great Britain and Northern Ireland (7/1/88)
   Bermuda (3/1/99)
   Cayman Islands (8/1/98)
   Falkland Islands (6/1/98)
   Isle of Man (9/1/91)
   Montserrat (3/1/99)
Venezuela (1/1/97)
Yugoslavia, Federal Republic of (12/1/91)
Zimbabwe (8/1/95)

Other countries may become party to the Hague Convention. When countries that are members of the Hague Conference on Private International Law do so, no formal action on the part of the United States is required for the treaty to come into effect. When nonmember countries become party to the Hague Convention, the United States must accept their accessions before the Hague Convention can take effect between the two countries.

Visit the Web sites of the Hague Conference on Private International Law (www.hcch.net) and the Department of State (www.travel.state.gov) for updates on additional countries party to the Hague Convention. You can also get this information by calling OCI or NCMEC.

Q: What is the Hague Convention's return remedy?

Subject to limited exceptions, Article 12 of the Hague Convention provides that a court must order the prompt return of a child under 16 who is wrongfully removed or retained within the meaning of the Hague Convention if less than a year has elapsed between the time of the wrongful removal or retention and commencement of the return proceeding.

Q When are removals or retentions "wrongful" under the Hague Convention?

A removal or retention is wrongful under Article 3 if it is in breach of custody rights that were actually exercised or would have been but for the removal or retention.

"Rights of custody" are defined in Article 5 to include "rights relating to the care of the person of the child and, in particular, the right to determine the child's place of residence." They are defined according to the law of the country in which the child was habitually resident immediately before the removal or retention. Custody rights may be exercised jointly or alone. They may arise by operation of law, court order, or agreement.

Q Do you need a custody order to seek a child's return under the Hague Convention?

No. You do not need a custody decree to invoke the Hague Convention. The Hague Convention recognizes that many abductions occur before custody has been decided by a court and provides the same return remedy in pre- and post-decree abduction cases. A Hague proceeding does not ask a court to enforce an existing custody judgment (which is what a traditional custody enforcement action entails), but rather calls upon a court to decide if a child's removal or retention was wrongful within the meaning of the Hague Convention.

An existing custody order may help foreign authorities determine if the removal or retention was in breach of custody rights and therefore wrongful, but it is neither required nor dispositive. As a practical matter, if you have a custody order, attach a certified copy to your return application.

In predecree abduction cases (i.e., when there is no custody order in effect at the time of the abduction), the searching parent may strengthen a future Hague Convention case by obtaining an order from a court in this country stating that the taking or retention of the child is wrongful within the meaning of Article 3 of the Hague Convention. Indeed, the foreign court hearing a Hague case may (pursuant to Article 15) request the applicant parent to obtain such a determination. In the absence of a judicial request—when it is not mandatory to obtain a determination of wrongfulness—you should consider how quickly and at what cost such an order could be obtained.

Q Are there any exceptions to the return obligation?

The Hague Convention provides limited exceptions to the return obligation:

- More than a year has elapsed and the child is now settled in the new environment (Article 12).

- The person seeking return was not actually exercising custody rights or has consented to or subsequently acquiesced in the removal or retention (Article 13(a)).

- There is a grave risk that return would expose the child to physical or psychological harm or otherwise place the child in an intolerable situation (Article 13b).

- A sufficiently mature child objects to being returned (Article 13).

- The child's return would not be permitted by the fundamental principles of the requested State relating to the protection of human rights and fundamental freedoms (Article 20).

Even if an exception is proved, courts retain discretion to order a child returned.

These exceptions have been interpreted differently by courts in different countries—and sometimes even by courts in the same country. Hague Convention case law is accessible at the following Web site: www.incadat.com. Make sure your lawyer knows about this site.

Q: Is there an official government office responsible for administering the Hague Convention?

Yes. Each country party to the Hague Convention must designate a central authority to carry out the duties specified in Article 7. The central authority for the United States (USCA) is the Office of Children's Issues in the Department of State. By contractual agreement, NCMEC acts on behalf of USCA in incoming Hague cases. NCMEC also provides assistance in outgoing Hague cases, including completing the return application. Keep in mind that many countries have not signed and ratified the Hague Convention and therefore do not have a central authority in place.

Q: What assistance does the U.S. Central Authority provide?

Although the central authority in the country where your child is located has primary responsibility for responding to your application, USCA can be helpful in a variety of ways. It is the primary source of information on the Hague Convention in the Federal Government. USCA can do the following:

- Provide you with a copy of the application used to seek return of the child (or enjoyment of access rights) under the Hague Convention.

- Review your application to ensure that it is complete and that your request complies with the requirements of the Hague Convention, forward it to the foreign central authority, and work with that authority until your case is resolved. (NCMEC will also work with you to ensure that your return application is complete.)

- Provide information on the operating procedures of the central authority in the country where your child is believed to be located and assist you in understanding the process.

- Provide you with contact information for the foreign central authority.

- Help you obtain (either directly or through NCMEC) information concerning the wrongfulness of the removal or retention under the laws of the State in which the child resided.

- Request a status report 6 weeks after court action commences in the other country if the court has not yet issued a ruling on your return petition. (*Note:* You should ask USCA to do this, because USCA does not routinely request status reports.)

- Facilitate communication between you and the other central authority. (*Note:* This does not include translating documents, which you must do at your own expense.)

- Provide information about a particular country's performance under the Hague Convention. Ask for this information! This is a good way to assess whether the Hague Convention remedy will work in your case. Some countries—such as the United Kingdom— are prompt in returning abducted children. However, the Department of State considers others to be noncompliant or not fully compliant under the Hague Convention and has identified others because they have inadequately addressed some aspect of their obligation. In the 2000 compliance report, the Department of State reports Austria, Honduras, Mauritius, and Panama to be noncompliant, and Germany, Mexico, and

Outgoing Hague Application

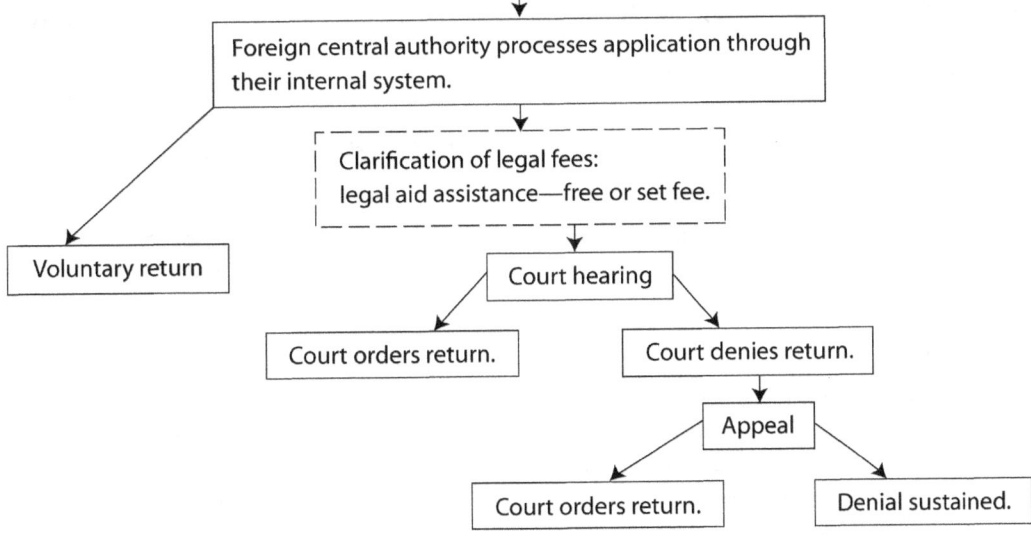

Sweden to be not fully compliant. Three other countries—Colombia, Poland, and Switzerland—are identified as not adequately addressing some aspects of their Hague Convention obligation.

Compliance information is available online. If you have access to a computer, go to the State Department's Web site (www.travel.state.gov), click on International Parental Child Abduction, and click on the two listed compliance reports. If a country has a poor track record under the Hague Convention, you should consider other lawful means to effect your child's return. Also consider strong prevention measures.

Also on the Web site is a report on the laws and procedures in 25 Hague Convention countries. This excellent resource provides a snapshot of how specific countries implement the Hague Convention.

How do you start a return action under the Hague Convention?

You have three options:

- Submit an application for your child's return to the U.S. Central Authority. USCA will forward the application to the foreign central authority.

- Bypass USCA and submit a return application directly to the central authority of the foreign country where the child is located. Address information for all foreign central authorities can be obtained from USCA. It is also available on the Hague Conference Web site (www.hcch.net). Follow the prompts for the International Child Abduction Convention, which is listed as #28 on their Web site. After filing the application, some cases may settle voluntarily. Others may be resolved administratively. In most cases, though, filing a lawsuit for return will be necessary.

- File a lawsuit directly with the foreign court, in which you request your child's return pursuant to the Hague Convention, bypassing both USCA and the foreign central authority. You are under no obligation to notify either central authority of your action, although you may do so and request whatever assistance those agencies can provide.

Do you need an attorney to bring a Hague action?

If you have to bring action under the Hague Convention in a court of the foreign country where the child is located, you will need the help of a lawyer in that country to do so. Central authorities in some countries may provide or arrange free or reduced-fee legal representation for applicant-parents. The U.S. Central Authority can inquire on your behalf about this possibility. Suggestions for finding an attorney in another country appear later in this chapter.

USCA will not act as your attorney or agent, nor will the Department of State become a party to your Hague proceeding.

Where can you get a return application, and is help available to fill it out?

You can use the application at the back of this guide. Cut it out or make a photocopy. The application can also be downloaded from the Department of State's Web site. Copies are also available from the U.S. Central Authority and NCMEC. NCMEC can help you prepare your Hague application and obtain supporting documents.

When should you start a return action?

Regardless of how you choose to invoke the Hague Convention, do not delay! File your return application as quickly as possible, and certainly before a year passes, if at all possible. There are two important reasons for acting promptly. First, the Hague Convention requires courts to return a child if less than a year has passed from the time of the wrongful removal or retention and the commencement of the return action, subject to limited exceptions. Second, once a return application is filed (or a court is put on notice of the abduction), courts and other authorities are not allowed to make substantive custody decisions about the child. This may prevent an abductor from getting a custody order in the foreign country.

Does the application have to be translated?

The answer depends upon the country involved. Submit your application in English. The U.S.

Central Authority can tell you whether your application must be accompanied by a translation and, if so, in what language. USCA does not provide or pay for translations. You can ask USCA or NCMEC for a referral to a translator.

If you seek return under the Hague Convention, can you continue trying to work out a voluntary return?

Yes, but be careful that your actions and conversations are not mistaken as acquiescence or consent to the wrongful removal or retention, which are defenses to return. Seek advice from your lawyer about how you can try to work out a solution with the abductor without jeopardizing your Hague Convention remedy should it be necessary.

Can criminal charges against an abductor impact a Hague proceeding for the child's return?

It depends upon the country.[1]

---

[1] According to a 1996 survey of foreign central authorities (contained in *Issues in Resolving International Child Abduction Cases* by Janet Chiancone and Linda Girdner of the American Bar Association Center on Children and the Law), seven central authorities reported that outstanding criminal charges have no effect upon whether they can proceed with a Hague return case. Of those that reported an effect, the impact of criminal charges varied. Sixteen central authorities reported that criminal charges are sometimes helpful in efforts to locate the child, and eight reported that criminal charges are sometimes helpful to proceeding with the case. Four central authorities reported that some judges in their country will not order a return if there are outstanding criminal charges, and one indicated that criminal charges must be dropped before judges can proceed with a case. Some courts have denied return under the Hague Convention when the abductor would face arrest on criminal charges if he or she accompanied the child home. Two other central authorities reported that outstanding criminal charges could "hinder voluntary return." (The study did not identify the respondents by name, so we do not know how particular countries responded.)

How can you find out if criminal charges will help or hurt a Hague case in a particular country?

You or your lawyer can ask the foreign central authority. Or your lawyer can research Hague Convention case law in the foreign country. You can consult with the U.S. Central Authority or with parents of children abducted to the same country about their experiences. (Team H.O.P.E. can match you with a parent.) But be aware that the issue may not have arisen in a particular country, so there may be no precedent to guide you.

What issues have arisen under the Hague Convention that you (and your lawyer) should know about?

The other country must be a treaty partner of the United States. The Hague Convention is not in effect between the United States and every country and therefore it may not be a remedy in your situation.

Compliance problems in some countries. Some foreign countries have a poor track record under the Hague Convention: courts have systematically denied return, and some countries have no procedures for enforcing a return order. USCA has compiled two compliance reports that identify countries with compliance problems (see "What assistance does the U.S. Central Authority provide?" on page 50). Your attorney should speak with the OCI case officers for the country in question for more information.

"Expeditious" handling isn't always so. The Hague process is supposed to be "expeditious." If a decision is not made by the court concerned within 6 weeks, you have the right to request an explanation for the delay. You can ask USCA to initiate such inquiry through the foreign central authority, or you can contact the foreign central authority directly. You are entitled to an explanation; however, there are no penalties for

slow decisionmaking. Further delay can be expected if an abductor appeals an order for return. Countries vary in how quickly courts have decided Hague Convention cases, ranging from extremely fast (United Kingdom) to very slow (Germany, Mexico, and Sweden).

Visitation. You can ask the foreign central authority to help arrange access pursuant to Article 21, either during the pendency of a return case, following the unsuccessful conclusion of a return proceeding, or instead of seeking return. However, this is the weakest part of the Hague Convention. The Hague Convention does not require "return" in access cases. This means that the court is not required to order the child to visit you in the United States. You should be prepared to go to the foreign country to see your child.

Even if a foreign court order provides for visitation, you may find that the abductor controls how and when you see your child, if at all.

—Tom Johnson

Hague return cases aren't supposed to be "best interests" hearings. Abductors may assert an Article 13b defense (grave risk of harm) to try to transform the return proceeding into a substantive custody trial. Your foreign attorney must be prepared to argue against allowing the abductor to litigate the merits of the case.

Undertakings. Courts in some countries (notably, but not exclusively, the United Kingdom) attach conditions (often referred to as "undertakings") to their return orders to protect the child until the courts of the country of habitual residence can issue orders concerning the child. For instance, a court may order a child returned (sometimes in the care of the abductor) but require the parent seeking return to pay for the child's—and abductor's—transportation, lodging, and support until a court in the country of habitual residence makes a custody decision.

Hague Convention may take precedence over International Parental Kidnapping Crime Act (IPKCA) charges. U.S. Attorneys may refrain from charging the abductor with an IPKCA violation during the pendency of a Hague proceeding.

Significant Public Benefit Parole. In some Hague Convention cases, courts have been reluctant to order a child returned when the abductor would be barred under immigration laws from entering the United States and thus from participating in custody proceedings. When these concerns arise, the foreign government may request that a *parole* be granted for the abductor for purposes of participating in custody or related proceedings in a U.S. court. The Department of State's Visa Office submits a request for *Significant Public Benefit Parole* to the Immigration and Naturalization Service, Parole Unit, which adjudicates (decides) the parole request. In addition to the possibility of parole for an ineligible alien, there is also the possibility of a waiver of visa ineligibility pursuant to section 212(d)(3)(A) of the Immigration and Nationality Act. A waiver requires the recommendation of the consular officer or the Department of State (Bureau of Consular Affairs/Visa Office) and the approval of the Attorney General (INS).

Q: Must you use the Hague Convention to seek your child's return?

No. The Hague Convention is not an exclusive remedy. You may seek the child's return using any other remedy available under the law of the foreign country. However, the Hague Convention probably is the best remedy in international parental kidnapping cases for the following reasons:

- You can apply for return even if you do not have a custody order.

- The U.S. Central Authority and the foreign central authority may be able to facilitate voluntary return or other resolution of the case.

- When an abductor learns that a Hague application has been filed, he or she may be more likely to return the child voluntarily.

- The foreign country may provide you with free legal representation.

Many foreign governments and legal systems have erected "pillars" that support abduction and retention: (1) extreme gender and/or national bias; (2) nothing comparable to contempt of court to enforce access, visitation, or return to the United States; (3) no principle of comity or respect for the laws and court orders of other countries; (4) payment of the abductor's legal fees and other expenses in their home country and the United States; (5) criminal legislation and law enforcement action to protect abductors; and (6) address protection to help abductors and children "disappear" These same pillars also come into play if the case ends up in a traditional custody proceeding in their courts. Some countries have all six pillars, while others have only a portion of them. But only one of the pillars may be necessary for a successful abduction/retention or for prevention of a left-behind parent in the United States from winning custody or visitation from a foreign court that exercises custody jurisdiction.
—Tom Johnson

- You may be able to recover attorneys fees and other expenses if the child is ordered returned.

- Courts are supposed to act expeditiously and can be asked to explain a delay after 6 weeks.

- Very few defenses are available, and even when proved, a court can order return.

- Foreign courts cannot make substantive custody orders concerning your child while the Hague action is pending.

Q: What happens if a foreign court denies return of your child under the Hague Convention?

You may try alternatives under foreign law to recover your child. A return decision under the Hague Convention—whether ordering or denying return—is *not* a decision on the merits of custody. Thus, a decision denying return should not be used against you in other legal proceedings in the foreign country.

Legal Solutions in Countries Not Party to the Hague Convention (and in Hague Countries, if You Do Not Invoke the Hague Convention or Return Is Denied)

Q: How can you find out what to do if your child is abducted to a non-Hague country?

Abduction cases to non-Hague countries remain the most difficult to resolve. Political, cultural, and religious differences between the United States and certain other countries may make recovery very difficult, perhaps impossible. Discuss recovery options with those most familiar with international kidnapping both in the United States and in the country to which the child was taken. Seek advice from your lawyer in the United States. You will probably also need an attorney in the foreign country to obtain authoritative advice on the laws of that country and to take legal action, if necessary.

Check with the Office of Children's Issues for information about the policies, procedures, and customs of the country in question. Ask OCI and NCMEC for information or documentation about recovery methods that have worked in the particular country. Talk to parents who have been in your shoes. Team H.O.P.E. can match you with a parent of a child abducted to the same country.

Before you get involved in litigation in a foreign court, consider trying to negotiate an out-of-court settlement with the abductor.

Can the U.S. Embassy represent you in legal proceedings in the foreign country?

No. U.S. consular and diplomatic officers are prohibited by law from performing legal services on behalf of U.S. citizens (22 C.F.R. 92.81). Thus, they cannot represent you, nor can they give you legal advice. They can, however, monitor the legal proceedings and provide other assistance, as described in the sidebar below.

What can the Office of Children's Issues (OCI) in Washington and the U.S. Embassy abroad do to help?

The Office of Children's Issues in Washington and the U.S. Embassy in the foreign country can provide information on the customs and legal practices in the country where your child is residing. They can also provide you with general information on serving process and obtaining evidence abroad, and authenticating documents for use in a foreign country. (See "The Role of the State Department in International Parental Kidnapping Cases" below.)

OCI can provide you with a list of attorneys in a foreign country who speak English, who may be experienced in parental kidnapping cases or family law, and who represent Americans abroad. (Other sources of lawyer referrals appear later in this chapter.)

Consular officers in the U.S. Embassy may be able to resolve communication problems with a foreign attorney. They may inquire about the status of proceedings in the foreign court, and

The Role of the State Department in International Parental Kidnapping Cases

What the State Department Can Do:
- In cases where the Hague Convention applies, assist parents in filing an application with foreign authorities for return of the child.
- Through U.S. Embassies and consulates abroad, attempt to locate, visit, and report on the child's general welfare.
- Provide the searching parent with information on the country to which the child was abducted, including its legal system and family laws, and with a list of attorneys there willing to accept American clients.
- Provide a point of contact for the searching parent at a difficult time.
- Assist parents in contacting local officials in foreign countries or contact them on a parent's behalf.
- List the child in a passport lookout database to alert the custodial parent of an application for a U.S. passport.
- Alert foreign authorities to any evidence of child abuse or neglect.

What the State Department Cannot Do:
- Reabduct the child.
- Help a parent to violate host country laws.
- Pay legal expenses or court fees.
- Act as a lawyer or represent parents in court.
- Give refuge to a parent involved in a reabduction.

they will coordinate with your attorney to ensure that your rights as provided under the laws of that foreign country are respected.

Q Will a foreign court enforce a U.S. custody/visitation order?

Maybe. If your child is abducted to a country that is not a party to the Hague Convention (or you are not using the Hague Convention), you can petition a court in the foreign country to enforce your custody order. A custody order issued by a court in the United States has no binding legal force abroad. However, courts in some countries may recognize and enforce a U.S. custody order on the basis of comity (the voluntary recognition by courts of one jurisdiction of the laws and judicial decisions of another). Comity is not mandatory.

Q What recourse do you have if a foreign court refuses to enforce your custody/visitation order?

If the foreign court refuses to honor a U.S. custody order, it may be necessary to file for custody or visitation in the foreign court under the laws and customs of that country. Foreign courts decide child custody cases on the basis of their own domestic relations law. They are not bound by U.S. law, although they may consider your U.S. custody decree as evidence. (See "Foreign Custody Jurisdiction" on this page.)

Q What if you don't have a custody order?

If you did not have a custody order at the time of the abduction or wrongful retention, a court in your State may still have jurisdiction to issue an order despite the child's absence from the State. Consult with a family law attorney to find out if it is still timely to file for custody. The applicable law is the Uniform Child Custody Jurisdiction Act or the Uniform Child Custody Jurisdiction and Enforcement Act. Under our legal system, the abductor must be given notice of your lawsuit. Your lawyer will need a foreign address for the abductor. If the abductor's whereabouts are not known, the law provides an alternative means of giving notice.

A custody order made after an abduction is sometimes called a "chasing order." Chasing orders may not be enforceable abroad, but there are reasons you may want to get one anyway. A custody order—even a temporary order—may be pivotal in getting law enforcement to investigate and prosecutors to prosecute. Importantly, once the child is returned, the order governs custody and visitation rights until modified.

Foreign Custody Jurisdiction

Q Under what circumstances will you have to litigate custody or visitation in the courts of a foreign country?

This can happen if you lose a return or access case under the Hague Convention, if a foreign court refuses your request to enforce a U.S. custody or visitation order, if you do not have a U.S. order to enforce, or if you have been advised to seek custody in the foreign courts.

Q What are the consequences of a foreign court exercising jurisdiction?

Although custody litigation in a foreign court may result in a child's return to the U.S.-based parent, this is by no means assured. Even if you were the child's sole caretaker before the abduction or wrongful retention, there is no certainty that you will be awarded custody. Foreign courts and authorities may give a home court advantage to an abductor who has returned to his or her country of origin with the child. You may also be at a disadvantage if the country has a cultural bias in favor of either the mother or father or if religious laws preclude an award of custody to you.

Even if you are awarded custody, there may be travel restrictions that interfere with the exercise of those custody rights. For instance, a Moslem husband's permission is usually needed for his children to leave an Islamic country, despite the fact that the children also have, for example, U.S. citizenship, and regardless of whether his non-Moslem wife has been awarded custody. The wife may also need her husband's permission to leave an Islamic country. Country-specific flyers and general information on Islamic family law are available on the State Department's Web site. Also, the National Center for Missing and Exploited Children has available a publication titled *Family Guide to Surviving Abduction to the Islamic World* that deals with international parental abduction in Islamic countries.

> Endless appeals and hearings in the other country, combined with a foreign government challenge all the way to your State supreme court of any custody order you have in the United States, are intended to exhaust your financial resources and to force you to give up.
>
> —Tom Johnson

If a foreign country grants you custody or visitation rights, there may be no legal mechanism in the foreign country to enforce compliance with the order. Under those circumstances, your victory may have been won at an excessive cost because the abductor keeps the child. If you lose custody, a foreign court will not necessarily award you visitation. If visitation is ordered, the child may not be allowed to come to the United States for visits; instead, you may have to travel to the foreign country to visit. Moreover, those visits may be restricted to a particular place or supervised.

Q Will you get a fair hearing?

This depends upon the country and its legal system as well as the facts of your case. Common law countries (in addition to the United States, Australia, Canada, Ireland, New Zealand, and the United Kingdom) are most likely going to provide a fair custody hearing. The common law evolved in England and is based largely on high court decisions in specific cases. Courts are bound by the legal precedent set by higher court rulings.

Civil law countries, which base their highly codified laws on Roman Law, do not provide the same kinds of due process protections or evidentiary rules that are basic to the U.S. legal system. Most countries of continental Europe and Central and South America have civil law systems. Whereas notice and opportunity to be heard are fundamental rights in U.S. custody proceedings, you may not be given adequate notice of proceedings in a civil law country. Nor may you be able to obtain the abductor's foreign address to serve notice of U.S. legal proceedings. Because civil law courts are not bound by precedent, case outcomes are less predictable than in common law countries.

Q Will you face discrimination based on gender or nationality?

In civil law countries (European countries, except Ireland and the United Kingdom) and others, you may face gender and/or nationality bias in the foreign courts. In Islamic countries, the children, at a certain age, come under the custody of the father or his family. For this reason, non-Moslem U.S. mothers do not fare well in Islamic courts in Middle Eastern countries. In other countries, partiality is shown to the parent from that country.

Q Will your child's wishes be considered?

Courts look to local law and practice to determine whether to consider a child's views. The law may set a minimum age, or it may contain vague standards. The Hague Convention is an example of the latter. Article 13 allows a court to refuse to order the return of a child if it finds that the child objects to being returned and "has attained an age and degree of maturity at which it is appropriate to take account of its views." The child's wishes are not dispositive—that is, courts may consider but are not necessarily bound by the child's stated preferences.

Q: If you are awarded custody or visitation, will the order be enforceable?

In many countries, parents who are awarded custody (sole or joint) or visitation may find it practically impossible to enforce the order if the abductor refuses to surrender the child. The country may lack laws and procedures to compel compliance. In the United States and a few other common law countries, civil court orders can be enforced through the court's civil and criminal contempt powers. If necessary, police action and incarceration of the offender can be used to enforce compliance. Judges in the vast majority of the countries of the world have nothing comparable to contempt power in civil cases. Judges in these countries cannot effectively enforce their own orders.

Q: Who pays?

Litigating in a foreign court can be a huge financial burden for searching parents. Travel, attorneys fees, and lost wages and income really add up. This is generally the responsibility of the parent. The abductor, on the other hand, may be subsidized in whole or in part by the foreign government.

You may pay in another significant way, too. Protracted litigation in the foreign country and in the United States tends to delay matters and to prolong the time the child and abductor are together. The longer the child stays with the abductor, the less likely it is that a foreign court will disrupt the relationship by ordering return.

Q: Do you jeopardize your legal position in the United States by pursuing custody or visitation in a foreign court?

Parents in the United States who pursue custody in foreign countries (when their Hague or enforcement action fails) run the risk that the foreign parent will then argue to a U.S. court that you have waived U.S. jurisdiction by participating in foreign proceedings. You can avoid this possibility by seeking an order from your home State court to the effect that your participation in foreign proceedings is totally without prejudice to your rights under U.S. law and to the validity of any U.S. custody orders you have obtained. Consult your attorneys in the United States and abroad to craft the best approach to protect and promote your interests in both countries.

Q: Can criminal charges in the United States against the abductor be helpful if civil proceedings abroad are not?

Possibly. Chapter 5 describes the advantages of using the criminal process in international parental kidnapping cases. It also examines reasons why the criminal process may not succeed with respect to a particular abductor (who may not be extradited for various reasons) or child (who is not the subject of a criminal process).

Children Abducted to Overseas U.S. Military Installations

Q: Are there any special remedies if the abductor is stationed overseas with the U.S. military?

Status of Forces Agreements generally protect members of the U.S. Armed Forces against

lawsuits (including those to enforce U.S. custody orders) brought in the civilian courts of the country in which they are stationed. You may, however, have an administrative remedy under Department of Defense (DOD) Directive 5525.9 (Compliance of DOD Members, Employees, and Family Members Outside the United States With Court Orders) (32 C.F.R. Part 146). This directive gives base commanders authority to enforce compliance with U.S. court orders concerning child custody or criminal parental kidnapping.

The directive requires the head of the overseas component (referred to here as "commanding officers") to cooperate with courts and with Federal, State, and local officials who request assistance in enforcing court orders against active-duty members of the Armed Forces, DOD civilian employees, or family members who accompany them. The directive applies to covered individuals who have been held in contempt for failing to obey a custody order, ordered to show cause why they should not be held in contempt, or charged with or convicted of a State or Federal felony (including parental kidnapping).

Military personnel on active duty overseas can be compelled to return to the United States to comply with court orders under circumstances described in the directive. Civilian employees, family members accompanying them, and family members of military personnel stationed overseas, while not subject to return, are encouraged to comply with court orders and face sanctions if they do not. Although the abducted child is not the subject of a return order or other sanctions, formal punitive measures taken against a parent may have a coercive effect that results in the child being returned to the United States.

If your child is abducted to or wrongfully retained on an overseas U.S. military installation, you should contact the base commander for help consistent with the directive discussed above. If your case cannot be resolved within the service member's chain of command, you can request help from the Department of Defense, Office of Family Policy, Support, and Services (see the "Directory of Resources" for contact information).

Finding a Lawyer

Q Do you need a lawyer?

In most cases, yes. International parental kidnapping cases are complicated. At a minimum, you will need a lawyer to navigate the legal system of the foreign country on your behalf. You may also need a lawyer in the United States.

Your U.S. lawyer may:

- Go to court on your behalf to obtain or modify a custody determination.

- Help you identify foreign counsel and assist your foreign lawyer, as needed.

Managing your resources correctly could make the difference between getting your child back and not getting your child back. A good expenditure of resources is on good sound legal counsel.
—Paul Marinkovich

- Help you in your dealings with law enforcement and prosecutors.

- Sue the abductor on your behalf for monetary damages.

- Seek better laws to address international parental kidnapping.

Your foreign lawyer may:

- Try to negotiate an out-of-court solution.

- Bring legal action for the child's return under the Hague Convention.

- Sue to enforce a U.S. court order.
- Sue for custody in the foreign court.
- Seek enforcement of a return order issued by a foreign court.
- Seek to arrange visitation between you and your child during the pendency of return proceedings, or afterwards if they are unsuccessful.
- Intervene with foreign law enforcement authorities for assistance in locating and apprehending the abductor.

Note that parents who are seeking the return of abducted children under the Hague Convention may be eligible for free counsel.

What should you look for in a lawyer?

Ideally, you want to find a lawyer who has successfully handled international parental kidnapping cases and whose fees you can afford. Your foreign lawyer should be conversant in English.

Where can you get referrals to lawyers who have handled international parental kidnapping cases?

Parents who have experienced the abduction of a child to a particular country are probably the best sources of referrals to lawyers and other helpful professionals in that country. Seek out similarly situated searching parents. Find out who their lawyers are and if they recommend them.

To find other parents who have had similar experiences, contact:

- National Center for Missing and Exploited Children.
- Team H.O.P.E.
- Your State missing children clearinghouse.
- Association of Missing and Exploited Children's Organizations.
- Department of State, Office of Children's Issues.
- The embassy of the country involved.

> When you ask another parent about an attorney and the response is something like, "I guess he was all right, but . . . ," this is definitely not the right attorney for you. When the response is something like, "Oh my gosh, you have to use this attorney because he is fantastic and takes these cases to heart," then you have found the right one and are ready for your interview.
>
> —Paul Marinkovich

Troubleshooting: Many missing children organizations and government offices are bound by privacy laws and policies and will not release the names of other parents without their permission. If you run into this problem, ask the agency to give your name and phone number to parents of children abducted to the same country, and ask to have those parents call you (collect, if necessary).

If you can't get an attorney referral from a parent with first-hand experience, other sources can give referrals to lawyers in the United States and abroad:

To find a lawyer in the United States, contact:

- American Bar Association, Section of Family Law, 312–988–5603, www.abanet.org/family/home.html.
- American Academy of Matrimonial Lawyers, 312–263–6477, www.aaml.org/.
- Local and State bar associations/lawyer referral services. Directories of State and local bar associations are available from the American Bar Association, 312–988–5000, and online at the ABA Web site, www.abanet.org/barserv. Some local bar associations list their referral services in the government listings in the telephone book.

- Department of Defense Legal Assistance Offices. If you are a member of the armed services or an accompanying family member, you may be eligible for legal assistance from the Legal Assistance Office for your branch of service.

- International Child Abduction Attorney Network (ICAAN). Maintained by NCMEC, ICAAN seeks to find attorneys in the United States to represent foreign parents in Hague Convention cases brought in U.S. courts. These same attorneys may be skilled in handling outgoing abduction cases and may be willing to take your case on a fee-for-service basis.

To find a lawyer in another country, contact:

- The Office of Children's Issues, which maintains lists of lawyers in other countries. In its capacity as the U.S. Central Authority for the Hague Convention, OCI can contact a foreign central authority on behalf of an applicant-parent in the United States to ask about the availability of free or reduced-fee counsel in the foreign country for a Hague Convention proceeding.

- NCMEC, which may be able to make referrals to counsel in other countries, although not necessarily on a *pro bono* or reduced-fee basis.

- International Academy of Matrimonial Lawyers, an association of lawyers in the United States and abroad with expertise in family law matters (www.iaml.org).

- International Law Committee of the ABA Section of Family Law (address above).

- Family Law Committee of the International Bar Association (IBA), a group of lawyers who handle international family law cases. Contact the current chairperson for referrals to lawyers in the United States and abroad (www.ibanet.org).

- Foreign bar associations. For links to all the major foreign bar associations, go to www.barassoc.org/Text/foreign_international.html.

What if you can't afford a lawyer?

- Look in the government pages of your local telephone directory under "Legal Aid" or "Legal Services Corporation" for the telephone number of the closest legal aid office. Call and ask if the office handles cases like yours. Many legal aid offices do not take family law cases. If yours doesn't, ask for a referral to the closest office that does.

- Local bar associations may provide reduced-fee legal services or may encourage attorneys to commit time to *pro bono* cases.

- Law school legal clinics in your area may assign law students to handle family law cases. They work under the supervision of the clinic director, who is typically a licensed attorney. Check your local telephone book for area law schools.

- Local battered women's shelters can sometimes help find affordable legal counsel.

- Parents' rights organizations (e.g., fathers' organizations, grandparents' rights organizations, and mothers-without-custody organizations) and similar groups may recommend lawyers to their constituents.

What questions should you ask before hiring a lawyer?

After you have identified a lawyer (or preferably more than one), call for an initial consultation. If it is convenient, go to the lawyer's office. If not, you can interview the lawyer on the telephone. Describe your situation and ask the lawyer about his or her relevant experience. Retain (hire) the lawyer only if you are comfortable with him or her and sense that the lawyer is equipped to handle your case. Be sure that the fee arrangement is acceptable to you. Consider asking for itemized bills. Interview another lawyer if necessary.

You can use the following list of questions for the initial interview. Adapt it for interviewing U.S. and foreign lawyers:

- How long have you been in practice?
- How many international parental kidnapping cases have you handled? How many Hague Convention cases?
- How many American parents have you represented in international parental kidnapping cases?
- How many of the cases resulted in the children being returned?
- How would you handle my case?
- Do you represent abducting parents?
- What are your fees and how do you request they be paid?
- Does your country have any legal aid provisions?
- Does your country pay the abductor's legal fees?
- What is your estimate of what my legal bill will be?
- Can you provide references of parents you have represented in similar cases? (Or you can ask the lawyer to have clients call you.)

Q What should you do if your lawyer isn't getting results?

If you lose confidence in your lawyer or if your lawyer isn't getting satisfactory results, discuss your concerns with him or her. Depending upon the direction your conversation takes, you may decide to discharge the lawyer and hire someone else to represent you. This can be a severe drain of time and resources, but it can also turn the whole case around.

Good legal counsel is a good expenditure, but the absolute best expenditure of resources is replacing ineffective legal counsel in midstream.... I have seen parent after parent struggle with attorneys who have not done the job. The most common thing I hear after the fact is that I wish I would have acted sooner.

—Paul Marinkovich

Child-Snatching Tort Suits

Q What are child-snatching tort suits?

Searching parents may sue abductors and others who assist them (e.g., grandparents, siblings, friends) for damages caused by the defendants' tortious (i.e., wrongful) conduct. The lawsuits seek compensation for out-of-pocket expenses and pain and suffering resulting from the abduction/concealment. They do not generally seek return of a child. However, the child may be located—and possibly returned—as a result of the lawsuit, either through the discovery process, which takes place after the suit is filed, or as part of a settlement with the defendant(s).

State law determines the causes of action, if any, that may be available in a child-snatching case. These include, but are not limited to, claims for unlawful imprisonment, interference with

custody or visitation, enticement, intentional infliction of emotional distress, outrageous conduct, and civil conspiracy. Child-snatching tort suits have been successfully brought in both State and Federal courts.

Q What kind of lawyer do you need for a child-snatching tort suit?

Your family lawyer may be able to bring a tort suit for you. However, you can also consult an attorney whose practice focuses on personal injury matters. Most tort actions are done on a contingency basis. This means that you do not pay legal fees to your attorney unless you win the case. The retainer agreement for the attorney's services normally specifies the percentage of the recovery that the lawyer keeps as compensation. Typically, you are responsible for filing fees and court costs.

Q Are child-snatching tort suits advisable in every case?

No, for a variety of reasons. First and foremost, you may be tired of legal battles. You may not want to get involved in another. From a legal standpoint, your State law may or may not recognize a cause of action for parental kidnapping, custodial interference, or the like. Even if it does, it may be futile to sue a defendant who would be financially unable to pay a judgment; you would recover little or nothing for your efforts. On the other hand, a well-founded lawsuit may serve as leverage to obtain the child's return.

If you decide against a child-snatching tort suit, there are other ways to seek recovery of your out-of-pocket expenses (i.e., the money you spent searching for your child, bringing legal action, paying lawyers, and going for counseling). Courts ordering return under the Hague Convention have authority to award attorneys fees and other expenses. (In the United States, they must do so *unless clearly inappropriate*.) Victim assistance laws (both State and Federal) may provide funds to left-behind parents if the abductor is criminally charged. At criminal sentencing, a judge can order an abductor to make restitution to you for some or all costs incurred in the location, recovery, and postrecovery treatment.

The Self-Help Dilemma

Q Do you have to use the foreign legal system, or can you personally get your child?

The Department of State strongly discourages taking desperate and possibly illegal measures to return your child to the United States. If you are contemplating such desperate measures, please consider not only the emotional trauma your child has already experienced as the victim of abduction, but the further trauma that may be inflicted by a reabduction. NCMEC also advises against reabduction, not only because it may subject the parent to criminal charges in the foreign country, but also because of possible psychological and physical harm to the child. Attempts to use self-help measures to recover an abducted child from a foreign country also may prejudice any future judicial efforts you might wish or need to make in the foreign country to stabilize the situation.

Q Can you be prosecuted abroad?

Possibly. Many countries closely regulate their borders and may maintain special lookouts for children likely to be reabducted. Depending on local law, a parent who is caught attempting a "snatch back" could be arrested and imprisoned in foreign jails. In imposing sentence upon a parent convicted of parental kidnapping (or other applicable law), a foreign court will not necessarily show leniency to a parent who had a custody order in his or her home country. A parent could be imprisoned or deported, which could preclude any future visitation with the child in the foreign country.

If you do succeed in leaving the foreign country with your child, you—and anyone who assisted you—may be the target of arrest warrants and extradition requests in the United States or any other country where you are found. Defending yourself against such proceedings is costly. Even if you are not ultimately extradited and prosecuted, an arrest followed by extradition proceedings can be very distressing for both you and your child.

Q: Will your child be safe upon return to the United States?

There is no guarantee that the chain of abductions will end once you return the child to the United States. Indeed, aggressive self-help may provoke another abduction.

Q: What are the risks of hiring someone to recover your child?

Not only is self-help legally risky and potentially traumatic, it can be expensive, especially if you hire a "commando" to recover your child. Talk to similarly situated parents if you are considering hiring someone who promises to recover your child. Team H.O.P.E. can put you in touch with another parent to share experiences and discuss your particular circumstances. While you may hear occasionally of a successful recovery, it is important to understand the numerous risks involved. You stand to lose the money you pay, which can be considerable. You may ruin any chance you have of lawful recovery or of securing access to your child in the foreign country. Your child may be traumatized by a failed recovery attempt, or even by a successful one. If your agent is unsuccessful, the abductor may hide the child to guard against another abduction attempt, your agent may face prosecution, and you may face liability as an accomplice.

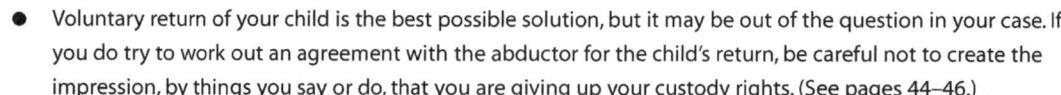

- Voluntary return of your child is the best possible solution, but it may be out of the question in your case. If you do try to work out an agreement with the abductor for the child's return, be careful not to create the impression, by things you say or do, that you are giving up your custody rights. (See pages 44–46.)

- If voluntary return is not feasible and your child is in a country that is party to the Hague Convention on the Civil Aspects of International Child Abduction, the Hague Convention is probably the best remedy for securing your child's return. You can also invoke the Hague Convention to try to exercise visitation with your child, although it has not proven to be particularly effective in "access cases." (See pages 47–55.)

- Legal solutions in non-Hague countries exist, but the results are not predictable and tend to vary by country. Some countries will enforce U.S. custody orders. In others, you may have to seek a new custody order. Courts in some countries grant custody based on the child's best interests. In others, the child's best interests are not paramount, and courts may base custody decisions on nationality, gender, or religion. Refer to the State Department's country-specific flyers, available online, for information about the custody laws of select countries. NCMEC's publication titled *Family Guide to Surviving Abduction in the Islamic World* addresses the issues of how to deal with international parental abduction in Islamic countries. (See pages 55–59.)

- Assistance may be available from a commanding officer if your child has been taken to or kept on an overseas U.S. military installation. (See pages 59–60.)

- Because of the complexities of international family law cases, you will most likely need to hire a lawyer in the foreign country and one in the United States. Some Hague Convention countries provide left-behind parents with free legal representation. (See pages 60–63.)

- In addition to taking legal action in a foreign country to recover a child, child-snatching tort suits may be brought in U.S. courts for money damages. These suits may incidentally result in a child's return. (See pages 63–64.)

- The State Department and the National Center for Missing and Exploited Children strongly discourage self-help recoveries. (See pages 64–65.)

NOTES

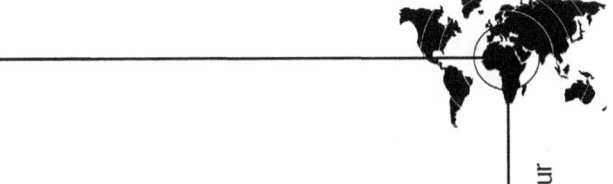

Chapter Four

5. The Crime of International Parental Kidnapping

International parental kidnapping is a crime under both Federal and State law. Specific provisions of State laws vary. Not every abduction or wrongful retention case will be covered by the applicable laws, nor will every case be prosecuted. Using the criminal process against international abductors has certain advantages, a key one being the ability of U.S. law enforcement to seek the cooperation of foreign authorities to locate and apprehend the abductor. Nevertheless, left-behind parents should consider a variety of issues before pursuing charges. For instance, very few countries are willing to extradite their own nationals. Even assuming that extradition of the abductor is possible, parents must be prepared to pursue other avenues to secure the child's return because the criminal process is aimed at returning the abductor and will not necessarily result in the child's recovery.

This chapter describes criminal parental kidnapping laws and explains how the criminal justice process works in international parental kidnapping cases. It should help you make an informed decision about whether to pursue charges and let you know what to expect if you do. Specifically, this chapter does the following:

- Provides an overview of the State and Federal criminal laws that apply in international parental kidnapping cases.

- Describes the roles of local law enforcement officials and prosecutors and their counterparts in the Federal Government—FBI agents and U.S. Attorneys—in investigating and prosecuting these cases.

- Explains the requirements for extradition and the reasons why extradition may not be a viable option in a given case.

- Points out the advantages and drawbacks of the criminal process.

- Raises issues for you to consider in deciding whether to file a criminal complaint against the abductor.

- Tells you how to proceed if you decide to pursue charges.

Frequently Asked Questions

State Crimes

What basics should you know about State criminal parental kidnapping laws and the criminal process?

What does your State parental kidnapping law cover?

Can accomplices be criminally charged?

What roles do local police and prosecutors play when an international parental kidnapping occurs?

Federal Crimes

What basics should you know about Federal criminal parental kidnapping laws and policy?

What is the Fugitive Felon Act?

What is the procedure for getting an Unlawful Flight to Avoid Prosecution (UFAP) warrant in an international parental kidnapping case?

What happens once a UFAP warrant is issued?

What is the International Parental Kidnapping Crime Act (IPKCA)?

Who is responsible for charging an abductor with an IPKCA violation, and how is the decision made?

Are there special charging considerations under IPKCA when children are abducted to or wrongfully retained in countries that are party to the Hague Convention on the Civil Aspects of International Child Abduction?

What charging considerations are there when children are abducted to non-Hague countries?

Who investigates an IPKCA violation?

Foreign Crimes

Can an abductor be prosecuted in another country?

Arrest

What happens to the abducted child when an abductor is arrested in a foreign country?

Extradition

What is extradition?

Is the child returned to the United States pursuant to the extradition of the abductor?

What are the prerequisites for extradition?

Conviction, Sentencing, and Crime Victim Assistance

What basics should you know about conviction and punishment?

Is victim assistance available to a left-behind or searching parent?

Pursuing Criminal Charges

Should you pursue charges against the abductor?

What are the advantages of criminal prosecution?

What else should you consider before seeking criminal charges against the abductor?

How do you pursue criminal charges against the abductor?

Troubleshooting

What myths hinder criminal prosecution and investigation, and how can they be dispelled? What are the realities?

What other practical problems are you likely to encounter, and what solutions are there?

What recourse do you have if the prosecutor declines to prosecute the abductor?

State Crimes

Q What basics should you know about State criminal parental kidnapping laws and the criminal process?

All 50 States and the District of Columbia have laws that treat parental kidnapping as a "felony" under specified circumstances. Generally, abductions and retentions that involve crossing State lines or leaving the country are felonies. Felony crimes are punishable by jail or prison terms longer than 1 year, payment of a fine, or both. Many States also have laws that treat parental kidnapping as less serious crimes, called "misdemeanors," under specified circumstances. Misdemeanors are punishable by incarceration in jail for up to 1 year, payment of a fine, or both.

Q What does your State parental kidnapping law cover?

Criminal parental kidnapping laws vary from State to State. Obtain a copy of your State's law by checking State criminal codes for applicable statutes either online or at your local library or law library. Such statutes are commonly called custodial interference, child abduction, child stealing, and parental kidnapping.

Copies of parental kidnapping laws may also be available from your State missing children clearinghouse, your local missing children's organization, your lawyer, the National Center for Missing and Exploited Children (NCMEC), and the American Prosecutors Research Institute (APRI). You can also check with the local police or prosecutor about applicable laws, although you may be more effective in dealing with law enforcement authorities if you already know what your State law provides.

Q Can accomplices be criminally charged?

Yes. Generally speaking, friends, relatives, and others who assist the abductor to abduct, retain, or conceal the child can be criminally charged as accomplices or co-conspirators. (However, just because they can be charged does not mean that they will be charged.)

Q What roles do local police and prosecutors play when an international parental kidnapping occurs?

Local law enforcement officers (e.g., your local police or sheriff) take reports of missing children and enter them in the National Crime Information Center Missing Person File (NCIC–MPF), as required by Federal law. The law also requires officers to investigate missing person cases. However, their ability to investigate cases that cross into foreign countries is limited. Law enforcement officers will coordinate with the

local prosecutor (e.g., the district attorney, county attorney, State's attorney).

The local prosecutor may charge the abductor with a crime, depending upon the circumstances of the abduction, the State criminal laws, and investigative input from local law enforcement. *Decisions to prosecute are made on a case-by-case basis by the prosecutor, who has discretion about whether and how to charge a case.* (This is called "prosecutorial discretion" and is exercised with respect to all criminal conduct.) When an abductor is charged with a State felony, the prosecutor may apply for a Federal Unlawful Flight to Avoid Prosecution (UFAP) warrant to bring the FBI into the investigation. (UFAP warrants are discussed below.)

Law enforcement and prosecutors may also have authority under State civil statutes (for example, the Uniform Child Custody Jurisdiction and Enforcement Act) to enforce custody determinations and to locate and recover abducted children—even if the abductor is not charged with a crime.

Federal Crimes

What basics should you know about Federal criminal parental kidnapping laws and policy?

Two Federal criminal statutes apply in international family abduction cases: the Fugitive Felon Act and the International Parental Kidnapping Crime Act.

It is FBI policy that the initiation of any criminal process in international parental kidnappings will be made on a case-by-case basis after considering all factors and the guidance of affected State and Federal law enforcement agencies, affected State and/or Federal prosecutors, the Departments of State and Justice, and the left-behind parent.

What is the Fugitive Felon Act?

The Fugitive Felon Act (18 U.S.C. § 1073) is a Federal statute designed to facilitate State prosecutions of State felony crimes. The Federal Parental Kidnapping Prevention Act of 1980 (PKPA) clarified Congressional intent that the Fugitive Felon Act applies to interstate and international abduction cases (18 U.S.C. § 1073 note).

What is the procedure for getting an Unlawful Flight to Avoid Prosecution (UFAP) warrant in an international parental kidnapping case?

First, the abductor must be charged with a felony under State law. Then the local or State prosecutor (*not* a left-behind parent) applies in writing to the U.S. Attorney or the FBI for a UFAP warrant pursuant to the Fugitive Felon Act. There must be evidence that the abductor has left the State or the country. A UFAP warrant usually will not be issued if the abductor's whereabouts are known, since the prosecutor can begin extradition proceedings without the help of the FBI. However, exceptions may be made in international abduction cases. The State prosecutor must give assurances that the offender will be extradited for prosecution.

For the FBI to assist with a UFAP warrant, the following criteria must be met:

- Probable cause must exist for belief that the abducting parent has fled interstate or internationally to avoid prosecution or confinement.

- State authorities must have an outstanding warrant for the abductor's arrest, charging him or her with a felony under the laws of the State from which the fugitive is fleeing.

- State authorities must agree to extradite and prosecute the fugitive from anywhere in the United States upon apprehension by the FBI.

- The local prosecuting attorney or law enforcement agency must make a written request to the U.S. Attorney for FBI assistance.

- The U.S. Attorney must authorize the filing of a complaint and the Federal arrest process must be outstanding prior to the time that the investigation was instituted.

Q What happens once a UFAP warrant is issued?

When a UFAP warrant is issued, the FBI investigates. An FBI agent in the United States coordinates an international investigation with the FBI Legal Attache stationed at the U.S. Embassy in the country to which the abductor has fled. Because U.S. authorities do not have jurisdiction in other countries, the FBI Legal Attache calls upon foreign law enforcement counterparts to continue the investigation with a view toward arrest and extradition. When arrested, the fugitive may return voluntarily to the United States or be extradited, pursuant to applicable treaties, to stand trial in State court on the State parental kidnapping charges. Under these circumstances, the Federal criminal charges under the Fugitive Felon Act would normally not be prosecuted.

The FBI's investigation pursuant to a UFAP warrant is directed at finding and returning the fugitive abductor. The child is not the focus of the investigation. If an abductor is located but the abducted child is not, the criminal investigation ends and the searching parent must continue the search. If foreign law enforcement counterparts discover the child's whereabouts during the course of an investigation to locate and apprehend the abductor, the laws and practices of the foreign country dictate what they do with the child. They may be authorized to take custody of the child, to alert local child welfare authorities about the child, to return the child to the left-behind parent, or to notify the left-behind parent to pursue recovery.

Q What is the International Parental Kidnapping Crime Act (IPKCA)?

In 1993, Congress passed the International Parental Kidnapping Crime Act (18 U.S.C. § 1204), making international parental kidnapping a Federal felony crime. IPKCA sends a strong message to the world that the United States views parental kidnapping as a serious crime. By enacting IPKCA, Congress also intended to deter abductions and to bolster efforts by U.S. diplomats overseas to secure the cooperation of foreign governments in returning abducted children to this country.

IPKCA makes it a Federal felony for anyone to remove a child under age 16 from the United States or to retain a child (who has been in the United States) outside the United States with the intent to obstruct the lawful exercise of parental rights. "Parental rights" are defined as the right to physical custody of the child, including visitation rights, whether that right is joint or sole and whether the right arises by operation of law, court order, or legally binding agreement of the parties. Violation of the statute is punishable by a fine, up to 3 years' imprisonment, or both.

The law provides three affirmatives defenses: the defendant (1) was acting within the provisions of a valid custody or visitation order; (2) was fleeing an incidence or pattern of domestic violence; or (3) failed to return the child because of circumstances beyond his or her control, notified or made reasonable attempts to notify the other parent within 24 hours, and returned the child as soon as possible.

Q Who is responsible for charging an abductor with an IPKCA violation, and how is the decision made?

The U.S. Attorney, usually in the district from which the child was taken, has authority to bring IPKCA charges in an international parental kidnapping case. *As in all criminal matters, decisions are made on a case-by-case basis, and the U.S. Attorney exercises prosecutorial discretion as to whether to charge a case.*

The U.S. Attorney will consider, among other things, whether State criminal charges are pending that could effectively resolve the case or whether IPKCA is the only charging option. Because of the broad definition of the Federal crime, some wrongful removals and retentions that do not fall under State laws may be covered by IPKCA. As a result, some cases can only be prosecuted under Federal law. For instance, IPKCA covers predecree abductions and visitation interference cases, whereas some State laws do not. If a case is charged under State law, IPKCA charges normally will not be brought because of the adequacy of the State law remedy. (An abductor can be extradited for a State felony as well.) However, there may be situations where the State may drop its prosecution in favor of Federal prosecution (for instance, if the State cannot afford to extradite the abductor). Such a decision would involve coordination between State and Federal prosecutors.

Q Are there special charging considerations under IPKCA when children are abducted to or wrongfully retained in countries that are party to the Hague Convention on the Civil Aspects of International Child Abduction?

The International Parental Kidnapping Crime Act expresses Congress's sense that, where applicable, the Hague Convention should be "the option of first choice for a parent who seeks the return of a child who has been removed from the parent." (The Hague Convention, an international treaty aimed at returning abducted and wrongfully retained children promptly to their country of habitual residence, is discussed in chapter 4.) If the abduction is to a Hague country, the U.S. Attorney will consider whether a civil remedy has been sought under the Hague Convention and whether a criminal prosecution under IPKCA (or any other State or Federal criminal statute) might adversely affect return proceedings.

An outstanding criminal warrant may deter a voluntary or negotiated return or may adversely impact a judge's decision to return a child under the Convention. Some foreign judges have been reluctant and others have refused to order a child's return if the abductor would be arrested on State or Federal charges on his or her return to the United States. This is not a unanimous view, however. Central authorities in eight countries have reported that criminal charges are sometimes helpful to a Hague proceeding. (See "Can criminal charges against an abductor impact a Hague proceeding for the child's return?" on page 53.)

Criminal charges may be appropriate when abductors violate Hague court orders and refuse to return the child. Also, an IPKCA warrant may be useful in locating and facilitating the return of a child. While the U.S. Attorney must be mindful of Congress's declaration that the Hague Convention is the preferred remedy for the recovery of a child who has been abducted to a country party to the Hague Convention, it is not a hard and fast rule. The left-behind parent should convey his or her wishes and concerns regarding a Hague Convention remedy in the case.

Q What charging considerations are there when children are abducted to non-Hague countries?

Many countries, including some Hague countries, do not recognize parental kidnapping as a crime, thus making international extradition unavailable. Nevertheless, IPKCA (or State) charges against the abductor may be useful in locating the abductor and child. INTERPOL alerts of various kinds may facilitate detection of the abductor's travel to another country from which extradition may be possible. The left-behind parent should continue his or her own efforts to recover the child even if the abductor is extraditable, because the child is not subject to extradition.

Q Who investigates an IPKCA violation?

The FBI investigates IPKCA violations, usually following a complaint by the left-behind parent. The FBI may open a preliminary investigation before criminal charges are formally brought. When an abductor is charged with violating IPKCA, the FBI investigates the case as an international fugitive felon matter.

As in UFAP investigations, the FBI's goal is to find and apprehend the abductor. If the child is located as a result of the investigation, the FBI does not physically return the child to the left-behind parent. Foreign authorities may assist in this regard, depending upon local law and practice, but parents must be prepared to arrange for the child's return.

Caveat: Congressional oversight hearings and a report by the General Accounting Office have revealed that very few abductors have been prosecuted under the International Parental Kidnapping Crime Act since its enactment in 1993. If you encounter difficulties in obtaining assistance from your local FBI or U.S. Attorney's office, additional steps you can take are suggested later in this chapter.

Foreign Crimes

Q Can an abductor be prosecuted in another country?

It is technically possible for a foreign country to prosecute an abductor under its own law for crimes committed in the United States.

Arrest

Q What happens to the abducted child when an abductor is arrested in a foreign country?

When an abductor is arrested for international parental kidnapping, only the abductor—not the child—is subject to return to the United States to stand trial. The laws and practices in the country where the abductor is arrested dictate what foreign law enforcement officers can do with the child when the abductor is apprehended. Foreign authorities may have authority to return the child directly to the left-behind parent or to otherwise facilitate that parent's recovery efforts. They may call upon local child welfare authorities to protect the child.

Do not assume that your child's return will be automatic, although you may be lucky in this regard. Be prepared to travel on short notice to resume custody and/or to participate in legal proceedings in the foreign country, if necessary. If there is a hearing, your presence may be pivotal.

If you cannot afford to travel abroad, financial aid may be available. With funding from the Department of Justice's Office for Victims of Crime, NCMEC provides financial assistance to parents who meet needs-based eligibility criteria so they can attend court hearings in foreign countries and/or transport their U.S. citizen children back to this country. The U.S.

Embassy abroad can arrange repatriation loans for U.S. citizens. Repatriation loans are subject to repayment.

Extradition

What is extradition?

International extradition is the means to return the abductor to the United States for prosecution under State or Federal law if the abductor refuses to return voluntarily. State and Federal prosecutors coordinate extradition through the Office of International Affairs (OIA), in the Criminal Division of the Department of Justice, which is responsible for pursuing extradition of wanted persons. Through INTERPOL and other international links, national law enforcement authorities in many countries regularly cooperate in the location and apprehension of international fugitives.

Is the child returned to the United States pursuant to the extradition of the abductor?

No. Extradition does not apply to the abducted or wrongfully retained child. It applies only to the abductor. While foreign authorities may facilitate return of the abducted child in connection with extradition of the alleged wrongdoer, there is no guarantee this will happen. Local law and practice, as discussed above, determine the child's fate.

What are the prerequisites for extradition?

State or Federal felony and a commitment to prosecute. State and Federal prosecutors must contact OIA at the outset of a case in which they intend to seek extradition. Either a State or Federal felony violation may serve as the basis for an extradition request, provided the maximum penalty meets the specific treaty requirement, usually 1 year or more of imprisonment for an extraditable offense. Extradition for both State and Federal prosecutors reflects a commitment to prosecute the abductor. The prosecutor must commit in writing to prepare the extradition request with supporting evidence; to pay the costs of extradition (translation and travel costs for escorts and the fugitive); and, assuming extradition is successful, to prosecute the abductor whether or not the child is returned.

Extradition treaty that covers parental kidnapping expressly or by mutual interpretation. For extradition to occur, the United States must have an extradition treaty with the country of refuge and the treaty partner must be willing to extradite persons, including its own nationals (if the abductor is its national), for international parental kidnapping.

The United States has more than 100 extradition treaties in effect. Some older treaties list the offenses for which extradition may be sought. These so-called "list treaties" include kidnapping, but do not expressly list parental kidnapping. Most were negotiated at a time when parental kidnapping was not widely viewed as a crime, either in the United States or abroad. To remove any ambiguity about whether the United States considers parental kidnapping a crime—which it has since 1993—Congress passed the Extradition Treaties Interpretation Act of 1998. The law authorizes the United States to interpret "kidnapping" in list treaties as including parental kidnapping. Extradition can occur only if the treaty partner also agrees to interpret kidnapping to include the kidnapping of a child by a parent.

The more modern extradition treaties to which the United States is a party contain "dual criminality" provisions, which provide for extradition when both parties have criminalized the conduct (i.e., where in each county the particular behavior that comprises the "kidnapping" is considered a criminal act).

Willingness of the requested country to extradite. Experience has shown that foreign governments and courts examine requests for extradition based upon parental kidnapping charges using factors that may not be explicitly defined in the treaty. Thus, decisions may be influenced by the extradition court's own investigation of the matter, by its judgement as to whether a civil resolution is possible—and preferred in a given case—or by domestic policy.

Conviction, Sentencing, and Crime Victim Assistance

Q What basics should you know about conviction and punishment?

If an abductor is convicted of parental kidnapping, it is very important for the victim-parent to ask the prosecutor to seek an appropriate sentence. Some States allow crime victims to be heard at sentencing, either in person (at the sentencing hearing) or in writing (through submission of a victim impact statement). Consult the prosecutor or probation officer about having your views heard.

Sentencing options include incarceration, probation, an order to return the child, and restitution. In lieu of incarceration (a jail or prison term), a judge may order probation, with conditions attached. For instance, the court may restrict the abductor's access to the child, prohibit out-of-State travel, or order the abductor to post a bond.

Caveat: Sentencing conditions last only as long as the criminal sentence; permanent changes in the custody order must be sought in family court.

When a State or Federal prosecutor secures a conviction against an abductor in an international parental kidnapping case, the prosecutor may seek conditions in the sentence that require the abductor to return the child to the United States. This type of condition was upheld in *United States v. Amer* (110 F.3d 873) (2d Cir. 1997). However, as that case illustrates, there is no guarantee such an order will accomplish its purpose.

Most statutes also allow the court to order the abductor to pay a fine as well as to make restitution to the victim for the costs of locating and recovering the child. If restitution is not specifically addressed in the parental kidnapping statute, State and Federal crime victim laws may authorize it.

Q Is victim assistance available to a left-behind or searching parent?

You may be eligible for crime victim assistance under State and/or Federal law. All States have enacted varying victim assistance laws that give crime victims certain rights and may also provide financial and other assistance. The Federal Victims of Crime Act (42 U.S.C. § 10,607) also provides rights and services to victims of Federal crimes.

For information on your State's crime victim program, contact one or more of the following agencies (contact information is in the Directory of Resources):

- Your prosecutor's office or State missing children clearinghouse, which should be able to tell you about crime victim programs in your State.

- National Center for Victims of Crime.

- National Organization of Victim Assistance.

For information on Federal victim assistance programs, contact:

- Department of Justice, Office for Victims of Crime.

For information on special programs to help the families of missing children, contact:

- NCMEC's Legal Department.

Pursuing Criminal Charges

Q Should you pursue charges against the abductor?

To answer this question, you should weigh the benefits of criminal prosecution against the impact it may have on you and your child.

Q What are the advantages of criminal prosecution?

A felony warrant may be the determining factor in the success or failure of locating the abductor, which in turn may lead to the recovery of your child. Some advantages of using the criminal process in international parental cases are listed below:

- Felony charges enable a prosecutor to issue a nationwide warrant for arrest of the abductor through the Wanted Person File of the FBI's NCIC computer. This improves the odds of detecting and arresting the abductor.

- If an abductor is a U.S. citizen and the subject of a Federal arrest warrant, the FBI or U.S. Attorney's Office can ask Passport Services at the State Department to revoke the person's U.S. passport. An abductor who is solely a citizen of the United States becomes an undocumented alien in a foreign country if the U.S. passport is revoked. Some countries may deport undocumented aliens or at least make it difficult for them to remain in the country.

Caveats: Passport revocation may not burden an abductor who is a dual national because the abductor may travel on a foreign passport. Passport revocation may interfere with negotiations for the child's return or with communications between the left-behind parent and child. Threatened revocation may cause the abductor to flee again with the child.

- Even if the abductor is not a U.S. citizen, the existence of a warrant may encourage the abductor to return the child voluntarily, especially if he or she has business or other reasons to travel to the United States. The warrant also serves to inform the foreign government that abduction of a child is a violation of U.S. law and that the abductor is a fugitive.

- NCMEC creates and disseminates posters of missing children in felony parental kidnapping cases and may facilitate Voice of America broadcast alerts for such children.

- State felony charges enable the prosecutor to seek a Federal UFAP warrant if the abductor has left the country. This warrant brings the FBI into the investigation. The FBI, in turn, can call upon foreign law enforcement to continue the investigation in the foreign country.

- Extradition is permitted for State and Federal felony crimes.

- INTERPOL may issue red notices when there is an outstanding felony warrant. Red notices put law enforcement worldwide on alert and may result in the abductor's arrest abroad.

- Federal and some State crime victim compensation funds provide monetary and other assistance (for instance, counseling) to left-behind parents and victim children.

Q What else should you consider before seeking criminal charges against the abductor?

Felony prosecutions of international abductors have clear advantages, but a decision to pursue criminal charges against the abductor requires careful consideration of the implications for you and your child.

Consider your goals. Presumably, your overriding interest is to obtain the return of your child, but this is not the prosecutor's primary responsibility. Apprehending, prosecuting, and punishing the abductor is. Because child recovery may be incidental to the government's pursuit of the abductor, you cannot rely on the criminal process to vindicate your custody rights or to get your child back. The prosecutor works on behalf of the public interest in having the State's criminal laws enforced. Your private attorney represents your personal interest in having your child returned and can go to court to seek to accomplish this for you. If you do not have a custody order, you must file a civil action in court to get one even if the case is being criminally prosecuted.

You must also keep in mind that neither extradition nor prosecution of the abductor guarantees the return of your child and may in some cases complicate, delay, or ultimately jeopardize return. Some judges have refused to order a child's return under the Hague Convention precisely because of outstanding criminal charges against the abductor in the child's country of habitual residence.

Consider whether you really want the other parent charged as a criminal. How will your child feel when the abducting parent is arrested, tried, or sent to jail? Will your child appreciate or resent your part in that process?

Consider the abductor's likely reaction to criminal charges. Some individuals might be intimidated enough to return the child. Others might go deeper into hiding, particularly if they have family or community support in another country.

Consider the prosecutor's control over criminal proceedings once they begin. Do not assume that you can stop the criminal process once charges are filed, if, for instance, the abductor promises to return your child in exchange for you dropping charges. Although the prosecutor may be willing to work with you, the prosecutor has the final say. Even if you change your mind about prosecuting the abductor, the prosecutor can proceed with the case.

Consider your potential role if the abductor is brought to trial. You and your child as well as other relatives and close friends may be called upon to testify. This will prolong your involvement with the criminal justice system and may make psychological recovery more difficult for both you and your child.

Consider the need to implement prevention measures regardless of whether the abductor is criminally prosecuted. A criminal conviction does not automatically restrict the abductor's visitation rights or provide long-term safeguards against a reabduction. Even if the judge imposes conditions in the sentence to minimize the risk of abduction, the restrictions remain in effect only for the duration of the sentence. You will have to go back to family court to make permanent changes in the custody order.

If you are determined to have the abductor criminally charged, prosecuted, and punished and are willing to assist the police, prosecutors, and court as requested, then it is appropriate for you to pursue criminal charges against the

abductor and accomplices. The next section explains how to go about it.

How do you pursue criminal charges against the abductor?

At the State level. Follow these steps to pursue State criminal charges against an abductor:

- Review your State's criminal parental kidnapping laws.

- Arrange a meeting with the local prosecutor's office. You may want to have your lawyer or a representative of a missing children's organization attend this meeting with you. If you have a custody order, bring a certified copy with you. (You can obtain one from the clerk of the issuing court.) Request felony charges against the abductor. If you cannot obtain a felony charge, ask for misdemeanor charges.

- Depending upon how the conversation goes, you might mention to the prosecutor that technical assistance on investigating and prosecuting parental kidnapping crimes is available at no charge from NCMEC's Legal Department and APRI's Child Abduction/Sexual Exploitation Unit.

At the Federal level. Follow these steps to pursue Federal criminal charges against the abductor:

- Contact the FBI Field Office nearest your home to request an investigation. Check the inside front cover of your local telephone directory for the number. Arrange a meeting with an FBI agent to discuss the abduction.

- Contact the U.S. Attorney's Office. Arrange a meeting—in person or by telephone— usually with an Assistant U.S. Attorney, to discuss the possibility of the Federal Government charging the abductor under the International Parental Kidnapping Crime Act.

Troubleshooting

What myths hinder criminal prosecution and investigation, and how can they be dispelled? What are the realities?

Too often law enforcement officers and prosecutors won't get involved in international parental kidnapping cases because of misconceptions they have about the crime. Refer to the discussion below if you encounter law enforcement officers who won't investigate or prosecutors who won't prosecute. But bear in mind that a prosecutor has the final say about prosecuting a case. You may be able to influence that choice by raising the profile of your case. See chapter 6 for suggestions on how to do that.

Myth #1. "It's a family matter." Some law enforcement officials and prosecutors are reluctant to intervene in a family abduction case because they view abductions as private family disputes, not criminal matters.

Reality. This view has been rejected by every State legislature in the country and by Congress, which have all passed laws making it criminal for a parent to abduct a child. You may need to show criminal justice system professionals the relevant State and Federal laws.

Myth #2. "Don't worry; your child is safe with the other parent."

Reality. Some law enforcement professionals have seen and written about the adverse toll kidnapping takes on young victims. If you encounter criminal justice professionals who are unaware of this, share with them the following passages, which are excerpted from *Missing and Abducted Children: A Law Enforcement Guide to Case Investigation and Program Management* (edited by Stephen E. Steidel, Arlington, VA: NCMEC, 1994):

> Research has begun to demonstrate what therapists and left-behind parents have

known for some time, that children are deeply and permanently affected by family abduction . . . . The emotional scarring caused by these events requires that officers recognize family abduction not as a harmless offense where two parents are arguing over who "loves the child more," but instead as an insidious form of child abuse. The history of the issue has also demonstrated that law enforcement has a much broader responsibility than the simple act of "retrieval." By responding promptly, professionally, and efficiently to reports of family abduction, officers and the agencies they represent become, in effect, a means of protection for the child . . . . (p. 67)

Parents have a right to look to the criminal justice system for assistance. To dismiss such pleas for help could push an anguished parent into desperate actions. Offering guidance . . . can avert potential domestic violence and snatch-back incidents. (p. 87)

Myth #3. "The U.S. Attorney says the Hague Convention takes precedence over IPKCA prosecution." A U.S. Attorney may refrain from charging an abductor based on the "sense of Congress" language in IPKCA, which says that the Hague Convention, where applicable, should be a parent's option of first choice.

Reality. The language section of IPKCA is not mandatory. Pursuing a Hague remedy is a parent's choice: it is often not the best remedy available, nor is it required. Delaying prosecution in countries where Hague proceedings are protracted or return orders are unenforceable may actually help the abductor succeed in keeping the child.

Q: What other practical problems are you likely to encounter, and what solutions are there?

Legal ambiguities. The prosecutor may be confused about whether a parent who abducts a child in violation of a joint custody order can be criminally charged. If your State's criminal law doesn't address joint custody, legal arguments can be made that a joint custodial parent who unilaterally takes a child without consent violates the other parent's joint custody rights. There is case law in some States to support this. Conflicting custody orders are another common source of confusion. Prosecutors and law enforcement officers are reluctant to take action when the parents have conflicting orders from different jurisdictions.

If your situation presents these or other issues, mention to the prosecutor that technical assistance on investigating and prosecuting parental kidnapping crimes is available at no charge from NCMEC's Legal Department and APRI's Child Abduction/Sexual Exploitation Unit.

Lack of resources. State and local prosecutors may not want to bring criminal charges or seek extradition in international parental kidnapping cases because of the considerable costs involved, including translating documents and transporting the abductor and escort officers back to the United States.

The cost of the criminal process clearly rests with the government. Nevertheless, parents have reported being asked by State or local prosecutors to pay these costs. If you find yourself in this predicament, you can agree to pay. But a more equitable solution may be available if the U.S. Attorney is willing to charge the abductor under IPKCA. The cost of extradition would then be borne by the Federal Government. The

local prosecutor can discuss the case with the U.S. Attorney. Normally, Federal charges will not be brought if State charges are already pending. However, the State prosecutor may be willing to drop State charges if the U.S. Attorney proceeds against the abductor.

Foreign governments that won't extradite. The prosecutor may be unwilling to charge the abductor if extradition efforts would likely be futile, for instance, because the abductor is a national of the country from which extradition would be sought and that country does not extradite its own nationals. Remind the prosecutor that felony charges can be helpful for many reasons even if the other country is unlikely to extradite its own nationals. For instance, when the whereabouts of the abductor and child are unknown, felony charges facilitate worldwide lookouts. Moreover, it should not be assumed that a foreign national has abducted a child to his or her home country. Even if this is the case, there is always the possibility of finding and arresting the abductor in another country from which extradition is possible.

Ask the Federal Government to intercede with the foreign government on behalf of your abducted child. Don't accept "no" or "it's a private custody dispute" for an answer. Remind [each person] that your child is an American citizen who deserves this great Government's protection. If a bank robber holds hostages, law enforcement officers do everything possible to remove the hostages to safety. Abducted children held hostage by their abductors deserve at least the same protection.

—Paul Marinkovich

Lack of experience. Resources are available to assist prosecutors and investigators who have little experience in these kinds of cases. State and local prosecutors may consult with APRI's Child Abduction/Sexual Exploitation Unit and NCMEC's Legal Department for technical assistance regarding investigation and prosecution of parental kidnapping crimes. The U.S. Attorney can get technical assistance on IPKCA prosecutions from the Department of Justice, Criminal Division, Child Exploitation and Obscenity Section, and on international extradition from the Office of International Affairs. FBI agents working on these cases can get help from the FBI's Office of Crimes Against Children (see the "Directory of Resources" for contact information).

Q: What recourse do you have if the prosecutor declines to prosecute the abductor?

First, seek review by senior prosecutors. If you have been meeting with a Deputy District Attorney, request a meeting with the District Attorney. If you have been meeting with an Assistant U.S. Attorney, ask to meet with the U.S. Attorney.

If you do not get the results you're looking for at that level, try to rally support for prosecution. Seek help from your State missing children clearinghouse or missing children's organization. Organize family members and religious and community organizations to begin a letter-writing campaign. Consider seeking media coverage of your child's abduction, emphasizing the need for criminal prosecution. Finally, elected officials may also be able to help. (Chapter 6 describes a variety of people and organizations that can help raise the profile of your case.)

More permanent solutions may be found by joining with other victimized parents to advocate for changes in the laws and in law enforcement policies. Contact NCMEC, your State missing children clearinghouse, and missing children's organizations in your State for suggestions on changing laws. Support enactment of the Uniform Child Custody Jurisdiction and Enforcement Act if your State has not yet passed that law. Among other things, this Act expands the options police and prosecutors have to respond to interstate and international abduction cases. Ask law enforcement agencies to establish procedures for responding to parental kidnapping cases. Request that local law enforcement officers and prosecutors participate in training courses on handling parental kidnapping and missing children cases.

- Your child's abductor may be criminally punishable under State or Federal law. Check your State criminal code for relevant State laws. The applicable Federal laws are the Fugitive Felon Act (18 U.S.C. § 1073) and the International Parental Kidnapping Crime Act (18 U.S.C. § 1204). (See pages 71–75.)

- Even if the abductor's conduct fits the elements of a State or Federal criminal statute, pursuing prosecution is not always the best approach to a case. A searching parent should weigh the pros and cons of prosecution before pursuing charges. (See pages 78–80.)

- Law enforcement officials and prosecutors may be reluctant to charge the abductor with a crime because of misconceptions they have about international parental kidnapping. Your task is to dispel these myths. (See pages 80–81.)

- You must continue your own efforts to recover your child even if the abductor is criminally charged and extradited. The child is not subject to extradition. You may find it necessary to go to court in the foreign country or to work out other arrangements with foreign authorities to recover your child after the abductor is arrested or extradited. (See pages 82–83.)

NOTES

Chapter Five

6. Other Resources To Help Resolve International Parental Kidnapping Cases

As you work through the civil and criminal justice systems to locate your child, resume custody, or arrange visits, you should be aware of other resources that may be able to help you accomplish your goal. In particular, this chapter describes the following:

- The National Center for Missing and Exploited Children (NCMEC) and the International Centre for Missing and Exploited Children (ICMEC).
- Parent advocacy groups.
- Media.
- Elected officials.
- Foreign embassies.
- Human rights organizations.
- Friends and family.
- International corporations.

What these resources have in common is the ability to raise the profile of your case, which in turn may lead to a solution.

Frequently Asked Questions

How can the National Center for Missing and Exploited Children help?

What is the International Centre for Missing and Exploited Children, and how can it help?

Are there any parent advocacy groups working on behalf of internationally abducted children?

How can the media—television, radio, newspapers, and magazines—help?

How can elected officials help?

How do you access the State Department's Web site, and what information does it contain about international parental kidnapping?

Can foreign embassies and consulates help?

How can the abductor's family and friends help?

Can U.S. companies doing business in the foreign country help?

Can human rights laws and organizations help?

Q: How can the National Center for Missing and Exploited Children help?

NCMEC's International Division provides a range of services to parents, attorneys, law enforcement officers and agencies, nonprofit missing children's organizations, and other individuals concerned with international parental kidnapping cases. The Center:

- Operates a toll-free hotline for parents of abducted children (who can call to register their cases and seek help) and for people who have information to report about an abducted child. The hotline operates around the clock every day of the year. Call NCMEC's local or toll-free number and ask to be connected to the International Division.

- Provides technical assistance, referrals, networking, and other resources to relevant organizations in the United States and abroad on international child abduction cases.

- Helps parents complete Hague applications in outgoing Hague cases (that is, children taken from the United States to countries party to the Hague Convention on the Civil Aspects of International Child Abduction).

- Handles applications in incoming Hague cases (that is, children abducted to the United States) on behalf of the U.S. Central Authority.

- Maintains the International Child Abduction Attorney Network (ICAAN) to help parents find *pro bono* or reduced-fee legal representation for Hague cases brought in this country. Although the ICAAN network does not formally include lawyers in other countries, NCMEC may be able to refer parents to foreign lawyers or to sources of referrals in other countries.

- Confirms but does not make NCIC–MPF (National Crime Information Center Missing Person File) entries for abducted children who are missing.

- Administers the Victim Reunification Travel Program, a cooperative project with the U.S. Department of Justice's Office for Victims of Crime and Office of Juvenile Justice and Delinquency Prevention that helps fund international travel to reunite parents who are financially unable to recover their children.

- Helps supply Voice of America, a worldwide radio network, with appropriate cases for multicountry broadcast as part of the Voice of America alert program.

- Networks law enforcement officers investigating cases involving the same country or region. NCMEC is also linked with 50 State missing children clearinghouses in the United States, INTERPOL headquarters in France, the Royal Canadian Mounted Police in Canada, Scotland Yard in the United Kingdom, the Belgian Gendarmerie, the Politie in the Netherlands, the Criminal Intelligence Division in Australia, and others.

- Networks parents whose children are in the same country.

- Maintains a Web site (www.missingkids.com/international), which posts information and publications about international parental kidnapping. The site also posts photographs of children abducted from the United States who are believed to be abroad.

- Collects and distributes the most up-to-date information on preventing family abduction to both Hague and non-Hague signatory countries; and provides technical assistance on best practices for the prevention of family abduction.

Q: What is the International Centre for Missing and Exploited Children, and how can it help?

ICMEC was established in 1999 as an issue advocacy organization. It does not manage individual cases.

The Centre's goals are to:

- Provide a coordinated international response to the issue of missing and exploited children.

- Build a global, Web-based network to disseminate images of missing children and information about them.

- Extend training resources and support worldwide reforms to protect missing and abducted children.

- Become the recognized leader on behalf of international child victims.

As of June 2001, 10 countries, including the United States, are officially online with ICMEC:

- Argentina: ar.missingkids.com (Policia Federal Argentina).

- Australia: au.missingkids.com (National Missing Persons Unit at the Australian Bureau of Criminal Intelligence, Canberra)

- Belgium: be.missingkids.com (Child Focus, Brussels).

- Brazil: br.missingkids.com (SOS Crianca, Brasilia and Sao Paulo).

- Canada: ca.missingkids.com (Royal Canadian Mounted Police).

- Chile: ch.missingkids.com (Policia de Investigaciones de Chile, Santiago).

- Italy: it.missingkids.com (Criminalpol, Direzione Centrale Polizia Criminale, Roma).

- Netherlands: nl.missingkids.com (Divisie Centrale Recherce Informatie, Zoetermeer).

- United Kingdom: uk.missingkids.com (New Scotland Yard, London and Hertfordshire Constabulary).

- United States: NCMEC's Web site, www.missingkids.com.

Q: Are there any parent advocacy groups working on behalf of internationally abducted children?

Yes. In addition to ICMEC and NCMEC's International Division, several parent advocacy groups and nonprofit organizations are working to raise awareness about international parental kidnapping and to get children back to the United States. For a list of organizations, contact the Association of Missing and Exploited Children's Organizations, Inc.

Advocacy groups press for resolution of individual cases and seek legislation in the United States and abroad to make international parental kidnapping a priority issue.

Q: How can the media—television, radio, newspapers, and magazines—help?

Coverage by television and radio stations, newspapers, and magazines can definitely raise the profile of an international parental kidnapping case. Widespread broadcast and publication of your child's photograph and information about the case may produce concrete leads about your child's location. Such publicity may also encourage public officials to take action on your child's behalf.

But media coverage is not for everyone. You should assess whether publicity is appropriate for your situation. Consider the views of two searching parents:

> The media are very important. Why? A lot more people watch the news and read the newspaper than read missing children flyers.... Any time town officials have an open meeting, be there. Tell your story because the media will be covering these meetings. The more attention you get, the better the chance of reaching someone who may know something or who may be in a position to help. — Ray Morrison

> Consider your individual situation: Could the media have an adverse effect on the recovery of or relationship with your child? Don't allow anyone to push you into media exposure if you feel it will have a negative effect. — Terri Beydoun

If you plan to seek media exposure in a case that is under investigation by law enforcement, discuss your intentions with the investigator. Make sure media exposure will not interfere with the investigation. Unlike a stranger abduction case, in a parental kidnapping case the suspect is known, and law enforcement authorities usually have numerous leads and other contacts to explore. Publicity at the wrong time could jeopardize the investigation.

When you contact the media, be prepared by having copies of recent photographs of your child and the abductor. Provide the numbers of any criminal warrants against the abductor and telephone numbers for local law enforcement. Identify politicians who are working on your case so they can be interviewed.

If your child's whereabouts are unknown, try to get media coverage in many countries or by media companies with worldwide reach, such as CNN. Ask NCMEC to send your child's name to Voice of America, which broadcasts multicountry alerts on missing children. If you narrow your search to a particular country, try to interest the media in that country in your child's story.

Troubleshooting: If you want media attention and can't get it, contact your State missing children clearinghouse or a missing children's organization for help. If a criminal warrant has been issued for the abductor, NCMEC can assist with the media.

Q: How can elected officials help?

Elected officials cannot secure your child's return directly, nor can they control how courts in the United States or abroad decide custody, visitation, or abduction cases. What they can do is raise the profile of your case, which may yield the results you want. For instance:

- They can make inquiries and intervene on your behalf.

- They can enact laws to improve the handling of and response to international parental kidnapping. For example, Congress enacted legislation (Section 2803 of Public Law 105–277, the Omnibus Consolidated and Emergency Supplemental Appropriations Act of 1998) requiring the State Department to report annually on country-by-country compliance with the Hague Convention. Compliance reports not only alert parents about problem countries, they also support State Department efforts to seek improvements from those countries.

- They can hold oversight hearings on issues and concerns relating to international parental kidnapping.

If you are having difficulty locating and recovering your missing child, contact your elected officials to see if they can help.

Continuously pressure the Federal Government for intervention. Four years had passed since my daughter had been kidnapped, 4 years in which I had no direct response from the U.S. Embassy in Beirut, Lebanon. Not one piece of correspondence that I had sent was ever responded to until Senator Jesse Helms wrote the American Ambassador and requested cooperation on my behalf. At the time the family in Lebanon had balked on their promise to let me see my daughter. After Senator Helms wrote his letter, an Embassy employee called my ex-sister-in-law and reminded her that under Lebanese law, I was guaranteed this right. I saw my daughter within days.

—Terri Beydoun

Q How do you access the State Department's Web site, and what information does it contain about international parental kidnapping?

Go to www.travel.state.gov and click on "International Parental Child Abduction," where you will find the following information:

- Office of Children's Issues.

- OCI division of responsibilities (a list of personnel and the countries they cover).

- International Parental Child Abduction Booklet.

- Application for Assistance Under the Hague Convention on the Civil Aspects of International Child Abduction.

- Text of the Hague Convention on the Civil Aspects of International Child Abduction.

- Legislation: International Child Abduction Remedies Act (ICARA).

- List of countries that participate in the Hague Convention on Child Abduction.

- Islamic family law.

- Child Passport Issuance Alert Program.

- Report: From the Law Library of Congress to the Senate Foreign Relations Committee on the Operation of the Hague Convention in [25] Other Countries, October 2000.

- Reports (2001, 2000, and 1999) on compliance with the Hague Convention on the Civil Aspects of International Child Abduction.

- Congressional Testimony: 10/14/99 Statement of Assistant Secretary Mary A. Ryan Before the Committee on International Relations, U.S. House of Representatives, on the Implementation of the Hague Convention on the Civil Aspects of International Child Abduction.

- Judicial education on international parental child abduction.

- Country-specific abduction flyers.

- Links to INTERPOL, the FBI, NCMEC, and the Hague Conference on Private International Law.

Q Can foreign embassies and consulates help?

If your child is taken to a Hague Convention country, most likely you will rely upon the Hague Convention and the U.S. and foreign central authorities that administer it to resolve the case. If your child is in a non-Hague country, you should consider contacting the embassy or consulate of the foreign country for help.

Keep in mind that nothing is conventional when dealing with non-Hague countries and the recovery of your child. In many of these countries the kidnapping of a child is considered a custody matter and not a criminal act. You may be admonished not to reabduct your child, because it would then become a criminal matter. Try to explain that you are seeking to establish communication with your child for the good of the child. Embassy officials may be sympathetic and may even help you find creative solutions.

Try to establish rapport with Embassy personnel who represent the country where your child resides. After 4 years of no contact with my daughter, I was given a personal interview with representatives of the Embassy of Lebanon. Although my daughter's kidnapping was not considered a criminal matter, the Ambassador suggested that Lebanese authorities investigate the family with whom my daughter resides and encourage them to let me see my daughter. If this action failed to get results, the Ambassador suggested that he try to contact an organization of Moslem women whose husbands were Parliament members. They might be willing to pressure the family into allowing me to visit my daughter. I had to guarantee that I would not try to abduct her. The Embassy's approach put the family on the "hot seat," but allowed them to save face without being viewed as criminals.

—Terri Beydoun

Q: How can the abductor's family and friends help?

Relatives and friends of the abductor can help in two important ways. First, they may have information about your child's location (see chapter 3), and second, they may serve as liaison between you and the abductor or between you and your child.

You are fortunate if you are on good terms with the people in the abductor's support network. If you aren't, attempts to communicate with them can be very draining. You may be vilified and blamed for being a bad parent. Try to ignore personal attacks. Don't be deterred from your goal of recovering or reestablishing a relationship with your child.

Be persistent in your attempts to communicate with your child. In time, it may pay off. I listened to my daughter's family scream and yell at me and tell me I would never see or talk to my daughter before being hung up on. I continued to call, write letters, and thank them for taking care of my daughter. I now can call and speak to my daughter at length.

—Terri Beydoun

Q: Can U.S. companies doing business in the foreign country help?

If the abductor or the abductor's family is affiliated in some way with a U.S. company doing business in the foreign country, consider asking the company to try to persuade the abductor to return the child. This is a long shot on the list of "leave no stone unturned."

Q: Can human rights laws and organizations help?

Maybe. Alleging human rights violations stemming from the abduction is another long-shot approach to seeking a child's return. Consult a lawyer in the foreign country to evaluate whether it is worth committing resources to this type of approach.

- "Leave no stone unturned" in your quest to recover or reestablish access to your child.

- The National Center for Missing and Exploited Children and the International Centre on Missing and Exploited Children are both excellent resources in international parental kidnapping cases. (See pages 88–89.)

- Parent advocacy groups and nonprofit organizations may be an effective voice for your child and for the cause of internationally parentally kidnapped children in general. (See page 89.)

- Media coverage in the United States and abroad can raise the profile of your case and perhaps bring about a solution. (See page 90.)

- Your elected officials can be effective advocates on your child's behalf. They can make individual queries about your case and sponsor legislation to improve the response to and handling of international parental kidnapping cases. (See page 90–91.)

- Foreign governments can be potential sources of help. (See page 91.)

- Human rights laws and organizations may work on behalf of abducted children.

- You may be able to prevail upon sympathetic relatives and friends of the abductor to help you reestablish contact with your child or mediate a resolution to the conflict. (See page 92.)

- U.S. companies doing business abroad may be able to persuade employees who are related to the abducted child to exert some influence over the abductor to bring about a solution. (See page 92.)

NOTES

7. Reunification

Reunification is both an end and a beginning. It is the long-sought end of the search and recovery process. At the same time, it is the beginning of a period of readjustment for the victim child, the left-behind parent, and the family as a whole.

This chapter highlights problems you may encounter during the reunification process. It covers:

- *What to do if your child doesn't have a passport.*
- *How to pay for your child's transportation back to the United States.*
- *Two ways to remove immigration barriers that may prevent your child (or the abductor) from returning to the United States.*
- *Psychological issues that may arise and ways to address them.*
- *Legal issues that remain after your child's return.*
- *Loose ends to tie up for closure.*

Frequently Asked Questions

Practical Issues

How can a child return to the United States if he or she doesn't have a U.S. passport?

Are funds available to pay for a child's transportation back to the United States?

What can be done if a foreign court orders a child's return to the United States, but the child (or the abductor) is not a U.S. citizen and is ineligible to enter the country?

Psychological Issues

What factors affect a child's adjustment?

Will counseling be needed?

Where can you get more information about the psychological aspects of reunification?

Legal Issues

What legal issues remain after a child's return?

Closure

What else needs to be done for closure?

Practical Issues

Q How can a child return to the United States if he or she doesn't have a U.S. passport?

If the child is a U.S. citizen without a passport, the U.S. Embassy abroad can issue a passport on a rush basis so that the child can return to the United States without further delay. Contact the foreign embassy or the Office of Children's Issues (OCI) in the State Department in Washington, DC, for prompt assistance. If you are able to pick up the child yourself and the child is on your passport, you do not need an individual passport for that child. Information for obtaining passports for minor children is available from OCI and on OCI's Web site.

Q Are funds available to pay for a child's transportation back to the United States?

It is not uncommon for a searching parent to exhaust his or her financial resources—and even go into debt—trying to locate and recover an abducted child. If you are in this predicament, financial assistance may be available to help pay for your child's transportation back to the United States. The U.S. Embassy in the foreign country can arrange a repatriation loan if you meet need-based eligibility criteria. In criminal parental kidnapping cases, victim-parents may be eligible for victim assistance funds through a program administered by the National Center for Missing and Exploited Children (NCMEC) and funded by the Justice Department's Office for Victims of Crime. Funds may also be available from this program for you to attend court hearings in the foreign country. In Hague Convention cases, the abductor can be ordered to pay the cost of return as well as other expenses you incur seeking recovery of your child.

Q What can be done if a foreign court orders a child's return to the United States, but the child (or the abductor) is not a U.S. citizen and is ineligible to enter the country?

Ironically, an abductor or child who is not a U.S. citizen may be ineligible to reenter the United States because of his or her immigration status. Two possible solutions exist. First, the foreign government may request that the Immigration and Naturalization Service grant Significant Public Benefit Parole for the abductor and/or child. Second, it is possible to ask the Attorney General for a waiver of visa ineligibility in accordance with the Immigration and Nationality Act. (These are discussed on page 53, "What issues have arisen under the Hague Convention that you (and your lawyer) should know about?")

Psychological Issues

Q What factors affect a child's adjustment?

Many variables affect how a child and family adjust to each other when they are reunified after an abduction. These include the length of time the child was gone; the child's lifestyle with the abductor; the extent to which the child was brainwashed against the searching parent or the United States; the memories the child has of the searching parent and family (which in turn depends upon the child's age at the time of the abduction and how much time has elapsed); the child's familiarity with the family to which he or she is returning (which could now include an unfamiliar stepparent and siblings); and religious, cultural, or linguistic differences that may have developed since the child was kidnapped. Some abducted children make a smooth transition back to their searching families, while others find it difficult to readjust.

Be patient. Show affection and convey a sense of security. Take precautions so it won't happen again.
—*Jose and Miriam Santos*

Q Will counseling be needed?

Your child may need psychological counseling to cope with his or her experiences and to reintegrate into the family. Among other things, your child may feel guilty about not contacting you or trying to come home. The child may be angry at you for not rescuing him or her sooner. Alternatively, the child may have developed a deep bond with the abductor and may feel angry at you for separating them or may feel guilty about the affection they share. Your child is probably confused about everything that has happened and the conflicting stories he or she has been told. Your child may feel like a stranger in a strange land, not at all like the beloved child you feel so happy to have back at home.

Family counseling can be very beneficial. The return of a long-lost child can be difficult for brothers and sisters who may not know or may have only faint memories of their returning sibling(s). It can also be stressful for a new spouse of the left-behind parent, who instantly becomes a stepparent upon the abducted child's return. This is a highly emotional time, one that may call for the services of an experienced professional counselor.

If your child is school age, talk with the school guidance counselor and explain what your child has been through. Find out what kinds of services are available. Give the counselor a copy of your custody order. Ask the counselor to instruct the faculty and school staff not to release your child to anyone without your express permission.

Q Where can you get more information about the psychological aspects of reunification?

Three publications address this topic. One is NCMEC's booklet, *Family Abduction: How To Prevent an Abduction and What To Do If Your Child Is Abducted*. (You can get a free copy of this publication by calling NCMEC or by visiting its Web site.) Another NCMEC publication, *Recovery and Reunification of Missing Children: A Team Approach*, edited by Kathryn Turman, may also be of interest. The psychological aspects of reunification are covered in *Obstacles to the Recovery and Return of Parentally Abducted Children*, edited by Linda Girdner and Patricia Hoff. This final report of a study conducted by the American Bar Association for the Office of Juvenile Justice and Delinquency Prevention can be ordered from the National Criminal Justice Reference Service (800–638–8736, or online at www.ncjrs.org).

Legal Issues

Q What legal issues remain after a child's return?

You may be facing additional custody litigation in family court and the prospect of being a witness in criminal proceedings against the abductor. Consult your attorney to review your legal situation promptly upon your child's return.

If you do not already have a custody order, you should file for one now. If you have a custody order, you may file an action to have it modified. For instance, you may seek a change of custody, changes in the abductor's visitation rights, or provisions to prevent a reabduction. (Prevention measures that can be included in custody orders are described in chapter 1.) You may want to consider a child-snatching tort suit, which is described in chapter 4.

You may be called upon by the prosecutor to testify against the abductor in a criminal trial. If the abductor is convicted, you may have an opportunity to testify in the sentencing phase of the criminal proceedings. You may also seek victim assistance funds if the abductor is charged with a crime. (Crime victim assistance programs are discussed in chapter 5.)

Closure

Q What else needs to be done for closure?

Notify every individual, law enforcement officer, organization, government office, and media contact you have worked with or sought help from that you have recovered your child. Thank them for their assistance.

Chapter Seven

- The State Department can issue a passport for a U.S. citizen child on an expedited basis to speed the child's return to the United States. (See page 96.)

- Funds may be available (in the form of grants and loans) to help transport a child back to the United States. (See page 96.)

- There are ways to remove immigration barriers so that a child or abductor who is ineligible to enter the United States can do so. (See page 96.)

- Just as no two abducted children have identical experiences, no two children will feel the same way upon their return to the left-behind parent and other family members. Be prepared for various emotional issues upon reunification, not only for the returning child, but for other family members as well. Be patient. (See pages 96–97.)

- Consult your attorney as soon as possible after your child returns. You may have to get a custody order or modify an existing one. You may also be called upon to testify in a criminal trial against the abductor. (See pages 97–98.)

- Let all the people who have helped you through the ordeal know of your child's return. That knowledge will allow them to turn their attention to other parents who are still trying to get their children back. (See page 98.)

NOTES

Recommended Reading

General Guides

General guides relating to international parental kidnapping are available from a number of sources. Materials from the following three offices are highly recommended.

- **The Department of State, Office of Children's Issues (OCI).** One publication that is of particular interest to parents is *International Parental Child Abduction* (July 2001, rev.). This document is available at no charge from OCI. It is also available online at www.travel.state.gov/abduct.html (click on "International Parental Child Abduction," and then on "International Parental Child Abduction Booklet").

- **The National Center for Missing and Exploited Children (NCMEC).** A publication that is of special interest to parents is *Family Abduction: How To Prevent an Abduction and What To Do if Your Child Is Abducted*. This document is available free of charge from NCMEC. It is also available online at www.missingkids.com (click on publications, then click on title). Another recent publication, titled *Family Guide to Surviving Abduction to the Islamic World*, deals with the impact of international parental kidnapping cases in Islamic countries.

- **The American Bar Association (ABA), Center on Children and the Law.** The ABA Center on Children and the Law has conducted extensive research on the civil and criminal aspects of parental kidnapping, much of which is accessible through the Center's Web site, www.abanet.org/child.

Prevention: Risk Factors and Personality Profiles

Several publications discuss the risk factors and personality profiles associated with international parental kidnapping and ways to prevent abductions from occurring.

- Chiancone, J., and Girdner, L. 1998. *Issues in Resolving Cases of International Child Abduction*. Final Report. Washington, DC: U.S. Department of Justice, Office of Justice Programs, Office of Juvenile Justice and Delinquency Prevention. (Contact the Juvenile Justice Clearinghouse at 800–638–8376 for information on obtaining a copy of this report.)

- Girdner, L., and Johnston, J.R. 1996. *Prevention of Family Abduction Through Early Identification of Risk Factors*. Final Report. Washington, DC: U.S. Department of Justice, Office of Justice Programs, Office of Juvenile Justice and Delinquency Prevention. (Contact the Juvenile Justice Clearinghouse at 800–638–8376 for information on obtaining a copy of this report.)

- Hoff, P. 2000. *Parental Kidnapping: Prevention and Remedies*. Washington, DC: American Bar Association Center on Children and the Law. Available on the Web site www.abanet.org/child.

- Johnston, J.R., and Girdner, L. 2001. *Family Abductors: Descriptive Profiles and Prevention Strategies*. Bulletin. Washington, DC: U.S. Department of Justice, Office of Justice

- Programs, Office of Juvenile Justice and Delinquency Prevention. (Available online at ojjdp.ncjrs.org/pubs/general.html #182788.)

- Johnston, J.R., and Girdner, L. 1998. Early identification of parents at risk for custody violations and prevention of child abductions. *Family and Conciliation Courts Review* 36(3):392–409.

- Johnston, J.R., Girdner, L.K., and Sagatun-Edwards, I. 1999. Developing profiles of risk for parental abduction of children from a comparison of families victimized by abduction with families litigating custody. *Behavioral Sciences and the Law* 17(1999):305–322.

- Johnston, J.R., Sagatun-Edwards, I., Blomquist, M., and Girdner, L.K. 2001. *Early Identification of Risk Factors for Parental Abduction.* Bulletin. Washington, DC: U.S. Department of Justice, Office of Justice Programs, Office of Juvenile Justice and Delinquency Prevention. (Available online at www.ncjrs.org/html/ojjdp/2001_3_1/contents.html.)

Effects of Kidnapping on Victim Children

The following publications examine the impact of international parental kidnapping on the child and family.

- Forehand, R., Long, N., Zogg, C., and Parris, E. 1989. Child abduction: Parent and child functioning following return. *Clinical Pediatrics* 28(7):311–316.

- Greif, G.L., and Hegar, R.L. 1993. *When Parents Kidnap.* New York, NY: The Free Press.

- Greif, G.L., and Hegar, R.L. 1992. The impact of parental abduction on children: A review of the literature. *American Journal of Orthopsychiatry* 62(4):599–604.

- Haller, L.H. 1987. Kidnapping of children by parents. In *Basic Handbook of Child Psychiatry*, Vol. 5, edited by J.D. Noshpitz. New York, NY: Basic Books, pp. 646–652.

- Hegar, R.L., and Greif, G.L. 1991. Parental kidnapping across international borders. *International Social Work* 34:353–363.

- Schetky, D.H., and Haller, L.H. 1983. Child psychiatry and law: parental kidnapping. *Journal of the American Academy of Child Psychiatry* 22(3):279–285.

Directory of Resources

American Academy of Matrimonial Lawyers
150 N. Michigan Avenue, Suite 2040
Chicago, IL 60601
312-263-6477
312-263-7682 (fax)
office@aaml.org
www.aaml.org/

American Bar Association, Center on Children and the Law
740 15th Street NW., 9th Floor
Washington, DC 20005-1009
202-662-1720
202-662-1501 (fax)
ctrchildlaw@abanet.org
www.abanet.org/child

American Prosecutors Research Institute
99 Canal Center Plaza, Suite 510
Alexandria, VA 22314
703-549-4253
703-836-3195 (fax)
www.ndaa-apri.org

Association of Missing and Exploited Children's Organizations, Inc.
167 Washington Street
Norwell, MA 02061
781-878-3033
781-878-0838 (fax)
ameco@dreamcom.net

Child Find of America, Inc.
P.O. Box 277
New Paltz, NY 12561
800-A-WAY-OUT (800-292-9688)
914-255-1848
914-255-5706 (fax)
www.childfindofamerica.org

International Bar Association
271 Regent Street
London WIB 2AQ
England
+44 (0) 20 7629 1206
+44 (0) 20 7409 0456 (fax)

National Center for Missing and Exploited Children and International Centre for Missing and Exploited Children
Charles B. Wang International Children's Building
699 Prince Street
Alexandria, VA 22314
800-THE-LOST (800-843-5678)
703-837-2122 (fax)
www.missingkids.com

National Center for Victims of Crime
2111 Wilson Boulevard, Suite 300
Arlington, VA 22201
703-276-2880
703-276-2889 (fax)
www.ncvc.org

National Organization of Victim Assistance
1757 Park Road NW.
Washington, DC 20010
202-232-6682
202-452-2255 (fax)
www.try-nova.org.

Professional Bail Agents of the United States
444 N. Capitol Street NW., Suite 805
Washington, DC 20001
800-883-PBUS (800-883-7287)
202-783-4120
202-783-4125 (fax)
www.pbus.com

Royal Canadian Mounted Police
Missing Children's Registry
877–318–3576 (toll-free)
www.childcybersearch.org/rcmp/
 registry.htmsystem

State Missing Children Clearinghouses
For a complete list of clearinghouses, call NCMEC at 800–843–5678, or check NCMEC's Web site, www.missingkids.com.

Supervised Visitation Network
2804 Paran Pointe Drive
Cookville, TN 38506
931–537–3414
info@svnetwork.net
www.svnetwork.net

Team H.O.P.E.
800–306–6311
www.teamhope.org

U.S. Department of Defense

Military Worldwide Locator Services
www.defenselink.mil/faq/pis/PC04MLTR.html

Office of Family Policy, Support, and Services
Crystal Square Four
Suite 302, Room 315
1745 Jefferson Davis Highway
Arlington, VA 22202–3424
703–602–4990

U.S. Department of Justice

Child Protection Division
Office of Juvenile Justice and Delinquency
 Prevention
810 Seventh Street NW.
Washington, DC 20531
202–616–3637
202–307–2819 (fax)
www.ojjdp.ncjrs.org/missing

FBI Office of Crimes Against Children
935 Pennsylvania Avenue NW.
Washington, DC 20535–0001
202–324–3666
202–324–2731 (fax)
www.fbi.gov
(See the front of your local telephone book for the number of your local FBI Field Office.)

Juvenile Justice Clearinghouse
P.O. Box 6000
Rockville, MD 20849–6000
800–638–8376
puborder@ncjrs.org
www.ncjrs.org

Office for Victims of Crime
810 Seventh Street NW.
Washington, DC 20531
202–307–5983
202–514–6383 (fax)
www.ojp.usdoj.gov/ovc

The following Department of Justice agencies are available to assist State and local law enforcement and prosecution agencies:

Child Exploitation and Obscenity Section
Criminal Division
1400 New York Avenue NW., Suite 600
Washington, DC 20530
202–514–5780
202–514–1793 (fax)

Office of International Affairs
1301 New York Avenue NW.
Washington, DC 20530
202–514–2621

U.S. National Central Bureau–INTERPOL
202–616–9000
800–743–5630
NLETS: DCINTER00
NLETS (via NCMEC): VA007019W

U.S. Department of State

Office of Children's Issues
CA/OCS/CI
Washington, DC 20520–4818
202–736–7000
202–312–9743 (fax)
202–647–3000 (automated fax: call directly from your fax machine)
www.travel.state.gov

Office of Passport Services
2401 E Street NW., Room H911D, SA–1
Washington, DC 20037
202–663–2430

U.S. Central Authority
Contact the U.S. Central Authority by calling the Office of Children's Issues.

Application for Assistance Under the Hague Convention on International Child Abduction

To invoke the Hague Convention, submit two completed applications for each child. The application form may be photocopied. Type or print all information in black or blue ink. Furnish as much of the information called for as possible, using an additional sheet of paper if you need more space. If you have further questions about the form, you may wish to refer to the text of the Convention. You may also call the Department of State's Office of Children's Issues (CA/OCS/CI) at 202–736–7000.

Translation of the supporting documents into the official language of the requested country may be necessary. Translations can speed up the overall process. Foreign attorneys and judges tend to respond more favorably to such documents. Ask CA/OCS/CI for more information about supporting documents.

You may fax your Hague application to CA/OCS/CI, fax number 202–312–9743. Send originals and supporting documents by mail, express mail, or courier service to:

Department of State
Office of Children's Issues
CA/OCS/CI
Washington, DC 20520–4818

Be sure to sign and date the application.

Note: These forms are also available from the U.S. Department of State, Office of Children's Issues, and can be downloaded from www.travel.state.gov/abduct.html.

U. S. Department of State
OMB NO. 1405-0076
EXPIRES 10-31-2003
Estimated Burden - 2 Hours*

APPLICATION FOR ASSISTANCE UNDER THE HAGUE CONVENTION ON INTERNATIONAL CHILD ABDUCTION

FILL OUT ALL SECTIONS ON BOTH SIDES
A SEPARATE FORM IS REQUIRED FOR EACH CHILD

Application for: ☐ RETURN ☐ ACCESS

I. IDENTITY OF CHILD AND PARENTS

CHILD'S NAME (Last, First, Middle)	DATE OF BIRTH (mm-dd-yyyy)	PLACE OF BIRTH

ADDRESS (At time of removal)	U.S. SOCIAL SECURITY NO.	PASSPORT/IDENTITY CARD COUNTRY: NO.	NATIONALITIES

HEIGHT	WEIGHT	SEX ☐ Male ☐ Fem	COLOR OF HAIR	COLOR OF EYES

FATHER | MOTHER

NAME (Last, First, Middle)	NAME (Last, First, Middle)

DATE OF BIRTH (mm-dd-yyyy)	PLACE OF BIRTH	DATE OF BIRTH (mm-dd-yyyy)	PLACE OF BIRTH

NATIONALITIES	OCCUPATION	PASSPORT/IDENTITY CARD COUNTRY: NO.	NATIONALITIES	OCCUPATION	PASSPORT/IDENTITY CARD COUNTRY: NO.

CURRENT ADDRESS AND TELEPHONE NUMBER	CURRENT ADDRESS AND TELEPHONE NUMBER

U.S. SOCIAL SECURITY NO.	U.S. SOCIAL SECURITY NO.

COUNTRY OF HABITUAL RESIDENCE	COUNTRY OF HABITUAL RESIDENCE

DATE AND PLACE OF MARRIAGE, IF APPLICABLE	DATE AND PLACE OF DIVORCE, IF APPLICABLE

II. PERSON SEEKING RETURN OF/ACCESS TO CHILD

NAME (Last, First, Middle)	NATIONALITIES	RELATIONSHIP TO CHILD

CURRENT ADDRESS AND TELEPHONE NUMBER	OCCUPATION

NAME, ADDRESS, AND TELEPHONE NO. OF LEGAL ADVISER, IF ANY

III. INFORMATION CONCERNING THE PERSON ALLEGED TO HAVE WRONGFULLY REMOVED OR RETAINED CHILD

NAME (Last, First, Middle)	RELATIONSHIP TO CHILD	KNOWN ALIASES

DATE OF BIRTH (mm-dd-yyyy)	PLACE OF BIRTH	NATIONALITIES

OCCUPATION, NAME AND ADDRESS OF EMPLOYER	PASSPORT/IDENTITY CARD COUNTRY: NO	U.S. SOCIAL SECURITY NO.

CURRENT LOCATION

HEIGHT	WEIGHT	COLOR OF HAIR	COLOR OF EYES

DS-3013 (formerly DSP-105)
11-2000

*SEE PRIVACY ACT AND PAPERWORK REDUCTION ACT STATEMENTS ON REVERSE

ADDITIONAL SHEETS MAY BE ATTACHED

OTHER PERSONS WITH POSSIBLE ADDITIONAL INFORMATION RELATING TO THE WHEREABOUTS OF CHILD

IV. TIME, PLACE, DATE, AND CIRCUMSTANCES OF THE WRONGFUL REMOVAL OR RETENTION

V. FACTUAL OR LEGAL GROUNDS JUSTIFYING THE REQUEST

VI. CIVIL PROCEEDINGS IN PROGRESS, IF ANY

VII. CHILD IS TO BE RETURNED TO

NAME *(Last, First, Middle)*	DATE OF BIRTH *(mm-dd-yyyy)*	PLACE OF BIRTH

ADDRESS	TELEPHONE NUMBER

PROPOSED ARRANGEMENTS FOR RETURN TRAVEL OF CHILD

VIII. OTHER REMARKS

SIGNATURE OF APPLICANT *(sign in blue ink)*	DATE *(mm-dd-yyyy)*	PLACE

PRIVACY ACT AND PAPERWORK REDUCTION ACT STATEMENTS

This information solicited on this form is requested under the authority of the International Child Abduction Remedies Act, Public Law 100-300. The primary purpose for soliciting the information is to evaluate applicants' claims under the Hague Convention on the Civil Aspects of International Child Abduction, advise applicants about available legal remedies, and locate abducted children.

The principal users of this information are offices within the U.S. Department of State's Bureau of Consular Affairs. The information will be used to assist in facilitating operations under the Convention and may be provided to governments of member countries, bar associations and legal aid services, local police, social service agencies, and parents. This information may also be released on a need-to-know basis to other government agencies, including foreign agencies, having statutory or other lawful authority to gain access to such information.

Furnishing your social security number, as well as the other information requested on this form, is voluntary. However, failure to submit this form or to provide all the requested information may result in delay in the processing of your application.

*Public reporting burden for this collection of information is estimated to average 2 hours per response, including time required fro searching existing data sources, gathering the necessary data, providing the information required, and reviewing the final collection. You do not have to provide this information requested if the OMB approval has expired. Send comments on the accuracy of this estimate of the burden and recommendations for reducing it to: U.S. Department of State (A/RPS/DIR), Washington, DC 20520-1848.

Instructions for Completing the Hague Convention Application

I. Identity of Child and Parents

Child's Name. The child's full name: last name, first, middle.

Date of Birth. Month/Day/Year.

Place of Birth. City/State/Country.

Address. Child's address in the country of habitual residence at the time of the abduction or removal.

U.S. Social Security Number. A nine-digit number: 000–00–0000 (if known).

Passport/Identity Card. Issuing country and passport or I.D. number (if known).

Nationalities. Include all nationalities of the child (e.g. U.S., Canadian).

Height. Feet and inches.

Weight. Pounds.

Sex. Male or female.

Color of Hair. Child's hair color.

Color of Eyes. Child's eye color (include color photo, if available).

Father

Name. Full name of father: last name, first, middle.

Date of Birth. Month/Day/Year.

Place of Birth. City/State/Country.

Nationalities. Include all nationalities.

Occupation. Usual or last known.

Passport/Identity Card. Issuing country and number (if known).

Current Address and Telephone Number. Include ZIP code as well as telephone and fax numbers for work and home.

U.S. Social Security Number. A nine-digit number: 000–00–0000 (if known).

Country of Habitual Residence. Of the father before the abduction or retention, particularly if different from that of the child.

Date and Place of Marriage and Divorce, if applicable. Indicate date and location of marriage and divorce of the parents of the child. It is important to clearly state the marital status at the time of the abduction or retention.

Mother

Name. Full name of mother of child: last name, first, middle (include maiden name).

Date of Birth. Month/Day/Year.

Place of Birth. City/State/Country.

Nationalities. Include all nationalities.

Occupation. Usual or last known.

Passport/Identity Card. Issuing country and number (if known).

Current Address and Telephone Number. Include ZIP code as well as telephone and fax numbers for work and home.

U.S. Social Security Number. A nine-digit number: 000–00–0000 (if known).

Country of Habitual Residence. Of the mother before the abduction or retention, particularly if different from that of the child.

Date and Place of Marriage and Divorce, if applicable. Indicate date and location of marriage and divorce, as applicable, of the parents of the child. It is important to clearly indicate the parents' marital status at the time of the abduction or retention.

II. Person Seeking Return of/Access to Child

This section is for information concerning the person or institution applying for the return of the child to the United States.

Name. Provide the full name of the person or institution asking for the child to be returned.

Nationalities. Of the requester.

Relationship to Child. Relationship of the requester to the child (e.g., mother, father).

Current Address and Telephone Number. Include home, work, and fax numbers.

Occupation. Of the requester (if a person).

Name, Address, and Telephone Number of Legal Adviser, if any. Include ZIP code as well as telephone and fax numbers. *Some of this information may be the same as that already given.*

III. Information Concerning the Person Alleged To Have Wrongfully Removed or Retained Child

The information about the abducting parent is needed to assist in locating the child. Please provide all requested information and any additional facts that may help authorities locate the child.

Name. Full name of parent who has abducted or wrongfully retained the child.

Relationship to Child. Relationship of the abductor to the child (e.g., mother, father).

Known Aliases. Any other names the abductor may use.

Date of Birth. Month/Day/Year.

Place of Birth. City/State/Country.

Nationalities. Include all nationalities.

Occupation and Name and Address of Employer. Provide any employment information that may be helpful in locating the abductor, such as usual type of work, potential employers, or employment agencies.

Passport/Identity Card. Country and number.

U.S. Social Security Number. A nine-digit number: 000–00–0000 (if known).

Current Location. Of the abductor in the country where the child was taken.

Height. Feet and inches.

Weight. Pounds.

Color of Hair. Abductor's hair color.

Color of Eyes. Abductor's eye color.

Other Persons With Possible Additional Information. Provide names, addresses, and telephone numbers of anyone in the country to which the child was taken who could give the Central Authority in that country information on the child's location.

IV. Time, Place, Date, and Circumstances of the Wrongful Removal or Retention

Provide the date, to the best of your knowledge, that the child left the United States or when the wrongful retention began. Include the place from which the child was taken. Describe the legal relationship existing between you and the abducting parent when the child was removed. What were the circumstances leading up to the removal or retention? How did you learn of the removal/retention? Did the other parent take the child during a scheduled visitation? Did the other parent take the child for what you believed would be a short visit and then inform you that they were staying? Did they purchase round-trip air tickets to show that they intended to return? Had you and your family moved to the other country, and then you decided to return to the United States?

Take this opportunity to tell your story. Try to anticipate what claims the other parent may make and provide your explanation.

Note: Do not limit yourself to the space provided on the form. Additional pages may be attached to fully narrate the circumstances. However, please be concise.

V. Factual or Legal Grounds Justifying the Request

Provide information and documentation establishing that you had, and were exercising, a right of custody at the time of the child's removal. Generally, a right of custody is created by a custody order when parents are divorced, or by operation of State law when parents are still married or were never married when the child was taken. As stated, the Convention defines "rights of custody" as including "rights relating to the care of the child and, in particular, the right to determine the child's place of residence." Thus, you may have a "right of custody" as defined by the Convention even if you do not have court-ordered joint or sole custody of the child.

Important: If there is no applicable court order, please provide a copy of the State statute, case law, or an affidavit of law prepared by an attorney that establishes your right of custody at the time of the child's removal. This provision of the law may sometimes be found in the estate and wills section of the State code. Remember, you are not attempting to show that you would have an equal right to obtain custody in a subsequent custody proceeding, but that you had and were exercising a right of custody when the child was taken.

SEND IN YOUR HAGUE APPLICATION IMMEDIATELY. Do NOT wait to get an order of custody. Orders issued after removal/retention are irrelevant in a Hague hearing.

VI. Civil Proceedings in Progress, if Any

Indicate any civil action (in the United States or abroad) that may be pending (e.g., custody, divorce). Name court and hearing dates.

VII. Child Is To Be Returned to

Name. Of person to whom child will be returned.

Date of Birth. Of person to whom child will be returned.

Place of Birth. Of person to whom child will be returned.

Address. Of person to whom child will be returned.

Telephone Number. Of person to whom child will be returned.

Proposed Arrangements for Return Travel of Child. Provide means by which you propose the child will return to the United States if this is ordered. For example, would you travel to pick up the child, or would someone go in your place? Is the child old enough to travel by him- or herself? Is there someone in the foreign country who could return with the child? Would the child travel by car, train, airplane? Be specific.

VIII. Other Remarks

State here whether you are applying for return or access under the Convention. You should include here any additional information that you believe may be pertinent to the Hague application.

Sign and date the application in black or blue ink.

Hague Application Checklist

(Check with country officer for specific requirements.)

- ○ **Application form (signed original, one for each child).** Note: Country may require use of special application form.
- ○ **Marriage certificate (if applicable).** May need to be certified copy.
- ○ **Birth certificate of child.** May need to be certified copy.
- ○ **Divorce decree (if applicable).** May need to be certified copy.
- ○ **Evidence of custodial right:**
    - ○ Custody order, or
    - ○ Copy of State statute, or
    - ○ Affidavit of law regarding presumption of custody under State law, or
    - ○ Article 15 determination by State court.
- ○ **Other pertinent court documents.**
- ○ **Photographs of abducting parent and child.**
- ○ **Statement regarding circumstances of removal or retention.**
- ○ **Other documents specifically required by receiving country** (e.g., Article 28 Statement, power of attorney to foreign central authority).
- ○ **Translations (if applicable).**
- ○ **Application for legal assistance (if applicable).**

Abduction Checklist for Parents

The following checklist is a modified version of the one that appears at the beginning of the State Department's publication International Parental Child Abduction *(11th ed., July 1997). It is intended to guide you on the type of information you need to maintain and the questions you need to ask as you continue to search for your child. You are encouraged to work with your local law enforcement agency to ensure that no stone is left unturned and that all information is collected that might lead to recovery of and reunification with your child.*

Instructions

Your situation is difficult, but there are things that you can do. This list assumes that you know or strongly suspect that your child has been abducted abroad to a country that is not *a party to the Hague Convention on the Civil Aspects of International Child Abduction. If the country is* a *party to the Hague Convention and your situation meets the requirements of the Hague Convention, you can submit the Application for Assistance Under the Hague Convention on Child Abduction, which is included in this guide.*

If you do not have a Hague case, complete this checklist in detail and forward a copy to the Office of Children's Issues (OCI) when you report the abduction of your child. It is critically important that you continue to update OCI on the status of any developments in your case. You should send OCI updated copies of this checklist when new developments occur. You can fax the checklist to 202–663–2674 or mail it to Office of Children's Issues, 2401 E Street NW., Room L–127, Washington, DC 20037. The telephone number is 202–736–7000.

Abduction Checklist for Parents and Their Law Enforcement Partners

About the Child

Child's name:_____,_____,_____(last, first, middle)

Child is currently located (if known): _____(name of country)

      Address:_____

      Telephone:_____

      Fax:_____

      E-mail:_____

Child's date of birth:_____/_____/_____(month/day/year)

Child's place of birth:_____

Is the child a U.S. citizen? Yes ○   No ○

Is the child a citizen of any other country? Yes ○   No ○

If yes, what country?_____

Child's U.S. passport number:_____

Child's other passports (country and number):_____

Date your child was abducted or wrongful retention began:_____/_____/_____(month/day/year)

About You

Your name:_____,_____,_____(last, first, middle)

Address:_____

Telephone:_____

Fax:_____

E-mail:_____

Your relationship to child: ○ Mother   ○ Father   ○ Other (specify)_____

About the Abductor

Abductor's name:_____,_____,_____(last, first, middle)

Last known U.S. address:_____

Address abroad (if known):_____

Telephone numbers (if known) U.S.:_____ Foreign:_____

Fax numbers (if known) U.S.:_____ Foreign:_____

Abductor's relationship to child: ◯ Mother ◯ Father ◯ Other (specify)_____

Is the abductor a U.S. citizen? ◯ Yes ◯ No

Is the abductor a citizen of any other country? ◯ Yes ◯ No

    If yes, what country? _____

Abductor's nationality:_____

Passport number(s) U.S.: _____ Other (country and number): _____

Legal Relationship Between Parents

Marital status: ◯ Married ◯ Divorced ◯ Never married ◯ Separated

Do you have a custody order? ◯ Yes ◯ No

Date custody order issued:_____/_____/_____(month/day/year)

If so, were you awarded: ◯ Sole custody? ◯ Joint custody? ◯ Visitation?

Was the abductor awarded: ◯ Sole custody? ◯ Joint custody? ◯ Visitation?

Does the custody order prohibit your child from traveling without your (or the court's) permission or restrict the child's removal from the country? ◯ Yes ◯ No

Name of issuing court(s):_____

    Address:_____

    Telephone:_____ Fax (if known): _____

    E-mail:_____

Do you have a certified copy of your custody decree? ◯ Yes ◯ No

Note: You may need to furnish proof of your custody rights at various stages in your search and recovery effort. Please submit a copy of your certified order to the State Department.

1. Preventive Measures

If you have an urgent case (abduction in progress), skip this section and go to #2.

○ Has your child's name been entered in the Children's Passport Issuance Alert Program?
  ○ Yes ○ No

○ If your child is a dual national, have you informed the embassy and consulates of the foreign country of your custody decree and asked them not to issue a foreign passport to your child?
  ○ Yes ○ No

  Country: _____

  Date foreign embassy/consulate(s) contacted: _____

  Name(s) of official(s) contacted:_____

  Address:_____

  Telephone:_____

  Fax:_____

  E-mail:_____

○ If your child only has U.S. citizenship, but the other parent has close ties to a particular country, have you informed the embassy and consulates of that country of your custody order and asked them not to issue a visa to your child? ○ Yes   ○ No

  Country:_____

  Date foreign embassy/consulate(s) contacted:_____

  Name(s) of official(s) contacted:_____

○ Have you obtained a free copy of the National Center for Missing and Exploited Children's book *Family Abduction: How To Prevent an Abduction and What To Do if Your Child Is Abducted*? ○ Yes   ○ No

○ Have you requested a prevention packet from NCMEC? ○ Yes   ○ No

2. Emergency Action: What To Do Right Away if an Abduction Is in Progress

○ Have you reported the abduction to your local police department? ○ Yes   ○ No

  Date police report filed:_____

  Name of police officer:_____

Address:_____

Telephone:_____

Fax:_____

E-mail:_____

Case file number:_____

○ Has your child been entered into the National Crime Information Center (NCIC) Missing Person File? ○ Yes ○ No

    NCIC record number:_____

○ What are the make, model, year, color, and license plate number of the vehicle the abductor may use to transport the child?

_____

○ Have local law enforcement authorities entered the abductor's vehicle into NCIC? ○ Yes ○ No

○ Has local law enforcement (or the FBI) contacted USNCB–INTERPOL to put appropriate law enforcement authorities on notice of the abduction? ○ Yes ○ No

○ What is the abductor's probable destination? _____

○ What airlines would the abductor potentially use to depart the United States?

_____

_____

○ Have you reported the abduction to the FBI? ○ Yes ○ No

    Date of report to FBI:_____

    Name of FBI agent:_____

    Field office:_____

    Telephone:_____

    Fax:_____

    E-mail:_____

    Case file number:_____

○ Have you reported your child missing to the National Center for Missing and Exploited Children? ○ Yes ○ No

    Date contacted:_____

NCMEC case officer:_____

NCMEC case number:_____

○ Do you have a valid passport in case you need to travel overseas?

    Your passport number:_____

    Is this a U.S. passport: ○ Yes   ○ No

    Country, if not U.S.:_____

    Date passport issued:_____

    Date passport expires:_____

    Place passport issued:_____

Note: Make a copy of your passport information page, in case you need to submit it.

○ If you did not have a custody order at the time the child was abducted, have you since obtained one granting you sole custody or prohibiting the child's removal from the country? ○ Yes   ○ No

3. The Search

○ If your child's whereabouts are known, have you asked the Department of State's Office of Children's Issues (OCI) to initiate a welfare and whereabouts (W/W) search for your child overseas? ○ Yes   ○ No

    Country in which W/W requested:_____

    Date written request submitted to OCI:_____

○ Have you tried to establish contact with relatives or friends of the abductor? ○ Yes   ○ No

    If so, list their names, addresses, telephone and fax numbers, and the dates contacted:

    _____

    _____

○ Has an "authorized person" (law enforcement official, prosecutor, or judge; *not* a parent) requested a search of the Federal Parent Locator Service database for address information on the abductor and child? ○ Yes   ○ No

○ Have you asked the principal of your child's school to notify you of any requests the school receives to transfer your child's school records? ○ Yes   ○ No

○ Have you asked the State official responsible for official records to flag any requests the agency receives for your child's birth certificate? ○ Yes   ○ No

○ Have you made a poster of your missing child? ○ Yes ○ No

○ Have you contacted State and Federal victim assistance offices? ○ Yes ○ No

    Date contacted: _____

    Name of person you contacted: _____

    Assistance for which you are eligible, if any: _____

4. After Your Child Has Been Located Abroad

○ Have you retained an attorney in the other country? ○ Yes ○ No

    Name: _____

    Address: _____

    Telephone: _____

    Fax: _____

    E-mail: _____

    Date of court hearing abroad: _____

○ Have you filed a Hague application for return? ○ Yes ○ No

    Date: _____

    Where: _____

○ Have you filed any other legal actions for your child's return? ○ Yes ○ No

    Date: _____

    Where: _____

    Describe the type of action: _____

5. Possible Criminal Remedies

If criminal remedies are sought, there are other issues or questions that will need to be addressed by your law enforcement agency. While these questions or issues are the responsibility of law enforcement, they are presented below to help you understand the process and keep you informed.

○ Is international parental kidnapping a crime in the State where your child resided at the time of the abduction/wrongful retention? ○ Yes ○ No

○ Has a State warrant been issued for the abductor's arrest? ○ Yes ○ No

    If yes, date issued:_____

    Warrant number:_____

    Name of crime:_____

○ Has a Federal warrant been issued for the abductor? ○ Yes ○ No

    If yes, date issued:_____

    Name of criminal offense:_____

    ○ Unlawful Flight to Avoid Prosecution (UFAP)

    ○ International Parental Kidnapping Crime Act (IPKCA)

○ Have the child and abductor's names been entered in the NCIC computer? ○ Yes ○ No

    ○ Missing Person File number:_____

    ○ Wanted File number:_____

    ○ Felony Vehicle File number:_____

    ○ Other:_____ File number:_____

○ Have the abductor's agents or accomplices been criminally charged? ○ Yes ○ No

    If yes, provide the names of the persons charged:_____

○ Have law enforcement officials requested USNCB–INTERPOL to alert appropriate authorities in other countries about the abduction? ○ Yes ○ No

    ○ Diffusions issued/date:_____

    ○ Yellow notice issued/date:_____

    ○ Blue notice issued/date:_____

    ○ Red notice issued/date:_____

○ If the abductor is a U.S. citizen and charged with a felony, have U.S. law enforcement officials taken action to revoke the abductor's U.S. passport? ○ Yes ○ No ○ Don't know

○ Is extradition of the abductor possible? ○ Yes ○ No

Has the U.S. Department of Justice requested extradition on behalf of a U.S. Attorney or State prosecutor? ○ Yes ○ No

    If yes, from what country:_____

    Status of extradition request:_____

Index of Frequently Asked Questions

1. Preventing International Parental Kidnapping

Why is it important to recognize the risk of international parental kidnapping and to put appropriate safeguards in place?..4

Are there warning signs that your child is at risk of international parental kidnapping? 4

What are the personality profiles of parents who may pose an abduction risk? 5

What can a court do to reduce the risk of international parental kidnapping? 6

How can you persuade a judge that prevention provisions are needed? 6

Where can you find information about the potential obstacles to recovering a child from a particular country? 7

If you have made the case for prevention provisions, how do you know which ones to request? 9

What kinds of prevention provisions can a court include in its order?...9

Apart from asking a judge to include prevention measures in a court order, what else can a parent do to reduce the risk of abduction?...13

2. Urgent Cases: Stopping an Abduction in Progress

Can an abductor be stopped from leaving this country? 20

What are the roles of the FBI, NCIC, and INTERPOL in stopping an abduction in progress and in international parental kidnapping cases generally? 20

Can an abductor be stopped at a foreign port of entry?..22

What should you do upon discovering an abduction in progress?...23

What is the next step if interdiction fails and the abductor succeeds? 23

3. Searching for Your Child

Where can you get help finding your child?..31

What legal consequences might you face if you don't find your child quickly? 31

How long should you keep searching?...32

4. Civil Remedies in International Parental Kidnapping Cases

Voluntary Return

Is voluntary return feasible? 44

Where can you get help to negotiate a voluntary return? 45

If the abductor agrees to return the child, what can the U.S. Embassy do to facilitate the return?........46

What are your options if voluntary return isn't possible? 46

The Hague Convention on the Civil Aspects of International Child Abduction (Hague Convention)

What is the Hague Convention on the Civil Aspects of International Child Abduction?......................47

Does the Hague Convention address visitation rights? 47

When did the Hague Convention take effect in the United States? 47

What is the International Child Abduction Remedies Act (ICARA)?..47

What countries are treaty partners of the United States? 47

What is the Hague Convention's return remedy? 48

When are removals or retentions "wrongful" under the Hague Convention? 49

Do you need a custody order to seek a child's return under the Hague Convention?..........................49

Are there any exceptions to the return obligation?..49

Is there an official government office responsible for administering the Hague Convention?...............50

What assistance does the U.S. Central Authority provide? 50

How do you start a return action under the Hague Convention? 52

Do you need an attorney to bring a Hague action? 52

Where can you get a return application, and is help available to fill it out?..52

When should you start a return action?..52

Does the application have to be translated?..52

If you seek return under the Hague Convention, can you continue trying to
work out a voluntary return?...53

Can criminal charges against an abductor impact a Hague proceeding for the child's return?............53

How can you find out if criminal charges will help or hurt a Hague case in a particular country?........53

What issues have arisen under the Hague Convention that you (and your lawyer)
should know about?..53

Must you use the Hague Convention to seek your child's return?...54

What happens if a foreign court denies return of your child under the Hague Convention?................55

Legal Solutions in Countries Not Party to the Hague Convention (and in Hague Countries, if You Do Not Invoke the Hague Convention or Return Is Denied)

How can you find out what to do if your child is abducted to a non-Hague country?..........................55

Can the U.S. Embassy represent you in legal proceedings in the foreign country?............................56

What can the Office of Children's Issues (OCI) in Washington and the
U.S. Embassy abroad do to help?..56

Will a foreign court enforce a U.S. custody/visitation order?..57

What recourse do you have if a foreign court refuses to enforce your custody/visitation order?..........57

What if you don't have a custody order?...57

Foreign Custody Jurisdiction

Under what circumstances will you have to litigate custody or visitation in the courts
of a foreign country?..57

What are the consequences of a foreign court exercising jurisdiction?..57

Will you get a fair hearing?..58

Will you face discrimination based on gender or nationality?..58

Will your child's wishes be considered?..58

If you are awarded custody or visitation, will the order be enforceable?..59

Who pays? 59

Do you jeopardize your legal position in the United States by pursuing custody or
visitation in a foreign court? 59

Can criminal charges in the United States against the abductor be helpful if civil
proceedings abroad are not? 59

Children Abducted to Overseas U.S. Military Installations

Are there any special remedies if the abductor is stationed overseas with the U.S. military? 59

Finding a Lawyer

Do you need a lawyer? 60

What should you look for in a lawyer? 61

Where can you get referrals to lawyers who have handled international
parental kidnapping cases? 61

What if you can't afford a lawyer? 62

What questions should you ask before hiring a lawyer? 62

What should you do if your lawyer isn't getting results? 63

Child-Snatching Tort Suits

What are child-snatching tort suits? 63

What kind of lawyer do you need for a child-snatching tort suit? 64

Are child-snatching tort suits advisable in every case? 64

The Self-Help Dilemma

Do you have to use the foreign legal system, or can you personally get your child? 64

Can you be prosecuted abroad? 64

Will your child be safe upon return to the United States? 65

What are the risks of hiring someone to recover your child? 65

5. The Crime of International Parental Kidnapping

State Crimes

What basics should you know about State criminal parental kidnapping laws and the criminal process? 71

What does your State parental kidnapping law cover? 71

Can accomplices be criminally charged? 71

What roles do local police and prosecutors play when an international parental kidnapping occurs? 71

Federal Crimes

What basics should you know about Federal criminal parental kidnapping laws and policy? 72

What is the Fugitive Felon Act? 72

What is the procedure for getting an Unlawful Flight to Avoid Prosecution (UFAP) warrant in an international parental kidnapping case? 72

What happens once a UFAP warrant is issued? 73

What is the International Parental Kidnapping Crime Act (IPKCA)? 73

Who is responsible for charging an abductor with an IPKCA violation, and how is the decision made? 74

Are there special charging considerations under IPKCA when children are abducted to or wrongfully retained in countries that are party to the Hague Convention on the Civil Aspects of International Child Abduction? 74

What charging considerations are there when children are abducted to non-Hague countries? 75

Who investigates an IPKCA violation? 75

Foreign Crimes

Can an abductor be prosecuted in another country? 75

Arrest

What happens to the abducted child when an abductor is arrested in a foreign country? 75

Extradition

What is extradition? 76

Is the child returned to the United States pursuant to the extradition of the abductor? 76

What are the prerequisites for extradition? 76

Conviction, Sentencing, and Crime Victim Assistance

What basics should you know about conviction and punishment? 77

Is victim assistance available to a left-behind or searching parent? 77

Pursuing Criminal Charges

Should you pursue charges against the abductor? 78

What are the advantages of criminal prosecution? 78

What else should you consider before seeking criminal charges against the abductor? 79

How do you pursue criminal charges against the abductor? 80

Troubleshooting

What myths hinder criminal prosecution and investigation, and how can they be dispelled?
What are the realities? 80

What other practical problems are you likely to encounter, and what solutions are there? 81

What recourse do you have if the prosecutor declines to prosecute the abductor? 82

6. Other Resources To Help Resolve International Parental Kidnapping Cases

How can the National Center for Missing and Exploited Children help? 88

What is the International Centre for Missing and Exploited Children, and how can it help? 89

Are there any parent advocacy groups working on behalf of internationally abducted children? 89

How can the media—television, radio, newspapers, and magazines—help? 90

How can elected officials help? 90

How do you access the State Department's Web site, and what information does it contain about international parental kidnapping? 91

Can foreign embassies and consulates help? 91

How can the abductor's family and friends help? 92

Can U.S. companies doing business in the foreign country help? 92

Can human rights laws and organizations help? 92

7. Reunification

Practical Issues

How can a child return to the United States if he or she doesn't have a U.S. passport? 96

Are funds available to pay for a child's transportation back to the United States? 96

What can be done if a foreign court orders a child's return to the United States, but the child (or the abductor) is not a U.S. citizen and is ineligible to enter the country? 96

Psychological Issues

What factors affect a child's adjustment? 96

Will counseling be needed? 97

Where can you get more information about the psychological aspects of reunification? 97

Legal Issues

What legal issues remain after a child's return? 97

Closure

What else needs to be done for closure? 98

About the Contributors

Jodi Carlson—Jodi's stepdaughter was abducted to Germany 7 years ago, where she remains with her German mother. Jodi and her husband have visited with the girl and find her alienated from them and her extended family.

Terri Beydoun—Terri remains separated from her daughter after 7 years. The child was abducted by her father and taken to live with her paternal aunt in Sidon, Lebanon. The father lives in Saudi Arabia. Although the father was criminally charged under the Federal IPKCA statute, he continues to live and work in Saudi Arabia without any harassment.

Jean Henderson—Jean had no contact with her son, who was abducted at age 8, for more than 5 years. His abductor-father managed to stay one step ahead of Jean's location efforts. She was reunited with her son only when his father, facing a terminal illness, surrendered himself to U.S. authorities. The boy was in Spain at the time.

Tom Johnson—Tom's daughter, a citizen of both the United States and Sweden, has been wrongfully held in Sweden by her Swedish mother since 1995. Her retention there is in express violation of a Virginia joint custody agreement and the Hague Convention. Tom's attempts to visit in Sweden have been unsatisfactory. Tom firmly believes that the mother, a government lawyer, has been able to thwart his efforts to recover his daughter largely due to the assistance she has received from the Swedish government.

John LeBeau—John's twin toddlers were abducted by their mother, a Danish citizen, from their home in Florida in June 1996. She took the children initially to Denmark and then—in violation of a Hague return order—to England. The abductor-mother was criminally charged under the Federal IPKCA statute, no doubt the result of John's relentlessness in seeking Federal intervention on behalf of his children. Facing possible extradition from the United Kingdom, the mother returned the children to the United States to John's custody in December 1998. John remains concerned about the possibility of a reabduction.

Steve McCoy—Steve's son and daughter were abducted to Colombia, where they have remained since 1992. The little visitation Steve has had with his children has been in Colombia.

Paul Marinkovich—Paul's son was abducted by his mother, a U.S. citizen. The boy was initially located in Sweden, but he disappeared again with his abductor-mother. He was later found in and recovered from Scotland pursuant to the Hague Convention. The boy was returned to Texas where custody proceedings were instituted.

Ray ("Perry") Morrison—Perry's son was abducted by his mother, a Mexican national, in December 1997. Although the boy is still missing, Perry believes his son is in Mexico. Perry's wife has been charged with criminal child abduction.

Jose and Miriam Santos—Jose recovered his abducted daughter from Syria after she had been gone a year. At the time of the recovery, she was in the care of the abductor's companion.

www.ingramcontent.com/pod-product-compliance
Lightning Source LLC
Chambersburg PA
CBHW080443110426

42743CB00016B/3258